GWEN STEFANI

First published in Great Britain in 2007
by Artnik
Artnik is an A Jot imprint
26 Thurloe Street
SW7 2LT
UK

© ARTNIK 2007

ISBN 978-1-903906-71-2

Design: Supriya Sahai
Editor: NIcholas Artsrunik
Pictures **Luke Seagrave: www.rock-city.co.uk**
        RETNA: www.retna.co.uk

Printed and bound by tHB in Czech Republic

GWEN STEFANI

BRANDON HURST

artnik

PLATINUM BLONDE LIFE

If there is one word that can be used to describe Gwen Stefani's talents, it is 'diverse'. For a woman who once feared that she had no direction or motivation, her life has been a blur of action. Not only that, but her successes have been staggeringly varied. From her early days as a shy backing singer with a struggling ska band in the late 80s, she has evolved into a stunning diva with her own platinum-selling solo album, a fashion line, the beginnings of a film career and a future as a happy wife and mother to look forward to.

Gwen's appeal is many-faceted. Part of it is simply down to her looks (which earned her a position at #22 in Stuff magazine's '102 Sexiest Women in the World', 2002). She is 5'6" with no additives, though in reality she is rarely seen without her platform soles (she's under few mistaken impressions about their importance: 'sometimes you have to sacrifice your performance for high heels'): Gwen is a tall, leggy blonde, with a skinny, toned figure and washboard abs that she maintains by rigorously and frequently working out. There is often more than a touch of the tomboy, too - a sassy, energetic presence that she often plays on by wearing unisex clothes. And yet there is no doubt, with her high cheekbones, spectacular figure and trademark platinum blonde meringue of hair, that she is all woman.

Though she often dresses the tomboy, she is equally capable of playing the 1940's movie star. 'I want to be a guy, but I want to wear a lot of makeup,' is how she puts it. 'Maybe I should be more of a tough chick. But I'm not. That's not me. I love makeup. I love getting my hair done. I love getting pedicures. I'm the furthest thing from a rock chick.' Apart from her looks themselves, there is the way she presents them – on stage and off it. There is just no getting around it: Gwen's in-your-face performances cannot be ignored. She sings alternately in a high-pitched, schoolgirl tones that might be expected from the likes of Minnie Mouse, then in a strong, confident voice with a great range. And, as if that wasn't enough, there is the dancing that goes with it.

Part of it is a shameless forwardness that some have equated with 'skank appeal' – a kind of upfront, audacious sexuality that almost borders on the obscene in its degree. And yet, for all her brazen gyrations, thickly applied makeup and, as Harper's Bazaar tactfully put it, 'blessed-virgin-in-ecstasy poses', it is not fair to describe her as trashy. Gwen can be a confusing mixture. On the one hand, she is the prim, proper Catholic girl whose parents tried to protect her from the corrupting influences of men until she was well into her twenties. On the other, she is the spitting, swearing hellcat who sings about the injustices of how women have to act for their own safety. She inhabits that narrow border between Madonna and whore, not falling into either camp but with a foot in each. As Newsweek wrote, 'One of the most endearing things about Stefani is the way she simultaneously apes both feminist and bimbo stereotypes.'

For such a paragon of brazen sexuality, however, Gwen is remarkably restrained in other areas. Whereas many other rock singers have to keep looking over their shoulders for the paparazzi, she has nothing in the closet worth them chasing. The best they can do is look for stories concerning her nearest and dearest – who happens to be pin-up Gavin Rossdale, so it's not such a difficult job – and turn out scandals-by-proxy. She is outspokenly anti-drugs and anti-promiscuity (having claimed to have notched up a grand total of 2 boyfriends herself, by the age of 37). Gwen Stefani is remarkably old, chaste and clean for a rocker.

That's not to say that she hasn't found other ways of expressing herself. Her heart-on-the-sleeve style is one of the things that has endeared her to millions of fans the world over; her song lyrics are very often a direct reflection of what is going on in her life, warts and all. Heart-breaking relationships, insecurities about her age and appearance, hope and then desperation for marriage and kids, and her status as a singer, all feature in their verses. If the subject matter seems a little too 'dear diary', it is more than offset by the attitude she brings to it. For every 'I'm on the verge of tears again' that she sings, there is a corresponding, 'Fuck you, I'm a girl' to balance it. Life and art for Gwen are inextricably linked, the one providing the inspiration for the other.

The duality is one that Gwen is hard pushed to explain herself. She fully recognises that there are tensions between the athletic, screaming creation of her stage persona, and the bubbly but sincere home-girl she can be when she

is not in performance mode. One element of the phenomenon is that a part of her never grew up, she thinks. She wasn't the most popular or good-looking girl at school, by any stretch of the imagination. 'I wasn't a cheerleader or in the choir. I didn't have loads of friends,' she remembers. Now, that memory sits uneasily with her status as an international sex symbol and multiple-platinum singer. She feels like a fraud, and wonders how long it will be before the rest of us catch on.

'I think I've been able to fool a lot of people because I know I'm a dork. I'm a geek,' she confides. But she's no Jekyll and Hyde; Gwen fully embraces who she is and enjoys what she does. Who she is on-stage is just as valid as the girl she is off it – though she's aware of the distinction. One magazine called it the 'Suzy Homemaker' and the 'Suzi Quatro' in her. 'I think that is definitely a part of me, but I don't think that I go around when I'm offstage saying "Fuck you, I'm a girl" and running all over the place. It's definitely two sides of my personality.'

In recent months, Gwen has graduated from being merely a star into something else. She has become one of the select new group of super-celebrities: a rare breed of icons who have the correct characteristics and who have achieved the necessary level of fame to transcend their origins and become not a singer, or an actor, but a personality in their own right. The personality then becomes a commodity, which can be used to sell any number of other products – effectively a brand name like Nike, Starbucks or Gap. In Gwen's case, anything from music and video to clothes and cameras have been marketed.

For some, such a move is tantamount to selling out – as many fans have accused her of doing. There is no doubt a degree of truth in that. Image is all-important nowadays: arguably far more so than talent. It is used to sell products by the big, multinational corporations whose brand-names count for more than the goods they promote. But it is also used to sell ideas; even politicians recognise the power of spin and image when it comes to the (often apparently less important) concerns of policy content.

Much as Gwen has been elevated to that new status, though, there is genuine talent underneath the carefully manufactured image. Long before her potential was realised and tapped, she was legitimately recognised as a musical genius and style icon in her own right. It is a shame that the publicity

machine that has launched her personality cult has resulted – as she fully realises – in her decreased contribution to the music that has her name on it. Perhaps, in the months and years to come, she will return to her roots with the ska band who first brought her to the limelight.

So, behind that façade, who is the real Gwen Stefani? This biography looks at the tragedies, joys, heartaches and successes she has experienced along the way, exploring the influences that have made her the singer, sex symbol and fashion idol so well known today by millions across the world.

JUST A GIRL

Gwendolyn Renee Stefani was born on October 3, 1969, in Anaheim, California – the Orange County. Her joint heritage is apparent in her name; her father, Denis Stefani, is an Italian-American, whilst her mother Patti claims Irish and Scottish descent. Despite growing up right next to Disneyland, life was quite normal for Gwen and her siblings (a sister, Jill, and two brothers, Eric and Todd). 'I grew up in a family that was so perfect in its way of being traditional – church every Sunday and four kids and we all get along – I was always in this little nest,' she remembers.

Raised Roman Catholic, her upbringing was pretty strict by most standards, though she does not resent it. 'My parents were, like, totally rad,' she says - 'rad', incidentally, being one of Gwen's favourite pieces of slang. The family was close, and she got on well with all of her brothers and sisters (her earliest memory is stealing Oreo cookies from the kitchen with her brother Eric, scooping out the filling and making a sticky ball out of it). Back in those days, Eric was her partner in crime and the driving force behind many of her escapades. Later, she would have him to thank for pushing her into stardom.

For someone with such in-your-face sex appeal and energy now, Gwen was a very shy child, who claims that she spent most of her time in her room (which was covered in posters of Marilyn Monroe and other Hollywood icons). At school, she says she always felt like the 'fat, dorky kid' – a label that has stayed with her ever since. Even today, she thinks she is fooling people, and that one day they will catch on and realise that she is still that same kid.

Performing ran in the family. Her parents had both been in a folk band called The Innertubes, mother Patti playing the autoharp (a zither-like instrument popular among folkies), with Dennis on guitar. Even her grandfather would later appear on two of No Doubt's videos and the cover to the Beacon Street album. Dylan was the preferred artist for the record player, something Gwen quickly grew tired of; at this stage, her own tastes ran to musical numbers from shows such as The Sound of Music, Annie, and Evita – though that would change in a few years when her brother introduced her to Madness. She also took ballet lessons at a young age, though one of her enduring childhood memories is of wetting herself in a class at the age of five, because she was too timid to ask to go to the bathroom.

Brother Eric seemed to be the musical one of the children, always waking Gwen up by crashing out something or other on the family's old concert-hall piano. He recognised his sister's abilities even back then, and drafted her into service as a singer. 'He was the one with all the talent,' she recalls. 'I was like Eric's little toy. He forced me to sing.' Eric, for his part, remembers it differently. 'I'd use the word "begged." I didn't take a whip to her. She had a great voice and she was really cute and had her own thing going.' Their first collaboration was on a song that young Eric had written, entitled, 'Stick It In The Hole'. Eric has always maintained it was about a pencil sharpener. 'My brother made me do it,' she says by way of excuse. She was used to following his lead unquestioningly. 'I had him, so I didn't have to do anything, you know?'

At school, Gwen was still the shy kid, though she increasingly came out of her shell as time went on. She attended Loara High School in Anaheim, where she joined the swim team (the origins of her childhood nickname, Frog). She was never a very academic child, and completely lacked direction for many years. 'I always thought of myself as really lazy because I was bad at school… Not that I was a bad girl, just that it was hard for me to learn. I couldn't even pay attention. I spent the whole fuckin' time drawing pictures. The bell would ring and I would be like, "Gosh the period's over?"' By the time she left school, she would still have little idea of what to do with her life, until Eric came to the rescue.

The origins of her athletic figure and perfect abs lie in this period – again, at least partly down to her parents. Worried that she was too chubby, Gwen got involved in soccer and water sports. 'It was mostly for fitness reasons,' she claims. 'My grandma was one of those really obese women – I think that really frightened my mom, you know?' At the age of twelve, she was put on a strict diet. 'It was out of my mother's love for me,' she said, but there were obviously some misgivings. 'I don't know if that's so good for a kid to be concerned over that so early. I think it's haunted me in a way.' Nowadays, she works out hard on a regular basis to maintain her toned body.

Her parents were also very protective, keen to shield her from any kind of sexual awakening. She remembers one occasion when the family went to see Flashdance. Before they left, Dennis and Patti lectured her and her siblings about the heroine's (a steel welder and exotic dancer) dubious morality. Perhaps due to her parents' puritanical strictness and this self-conscious streak, Gwen rarely dated at school. Feeling 'dorky and fat', she would always turn boys down. 'The only line I ever used was, "I have a boyfriend",' she told *Female First*. 'I loved that excuse.' Occasionally, she would need more than an excuse. She remembers one boy from her band practice class who wouldn't take no for an answer. 'Every day I would just be fighting him off,' she remembers. Jill, her younger sister, remembers that she was better at dealing with other people's problems; Gwen was 'always giving really good advice about guys and about friends and about the superficiality of it all.'

She was well into her teens before her first kiss. Even now, she claims to bear a grudge against the boy. 'I was in the ninth grade, and I kissed this boy – Brad. I didn't even know his last name. It was on a family trip to Catalina Island in California. We kissed on the beach, and I remember thinking, "Oh my God, this is so weird. I can feel his braces!" My family left the next day. I wrote to him three times but he never wrote back.' In the light of this rejection, Gwen told *Contact Music* that she secretly hoped he regretted ignoring her, now that she was a superstar. Gwen's strict upbringing and parents' Catholic values have generally stayed with her, throughout her rise through the ranks and temptations of the entertainment business. 'Luckily we never had any troubles with her drinking or taking drugs,' her father says. 'She's serious about doing the rock-star thing as a profession, as opposed to "let's go party".'

Gwen lived at home for a long time after she finished school, and her parents continued to impose these values on her until she was into her twenties. When she graduated, instead of the usual parties that everyone else was having, Gwen had to go to Disneyland. A condition of the trip was that she had to be home by midnight. At the age of 21, she remembers a family holiday to Italy, where her father hailed from. 'It was like strict rules,' Gwen recalls. 'We're going there to see the churches and the art, and you can't talk to boys, and you have to wear long dresses with your shoulders covered.'

Wicked Style

One way that Gwen did learn to express herself was in her clothing. Again, her family provided the background for this obsession, for which she is today steadily gaining acclaim on the catwalk. Her mother and grandmother always used to make their own clothes, and Gwen soon began to follow suit. As a child, she remembers how she loved to dress up with her sister, Jill, and play with Barbie (even at that age, she had a keen interest in fashion and aspirations towards an unreasonably high-maintenance figure). Her parents unwittingly provided the stimulus for the bizarre and eye-catching outfits for which she has become so well known. Keen to shield her from any kind of untoward influence, they made sure that she wore white underwear until she went to high school. 'But when I hit puberty,' she remembers, 'I said, "OK, I'm going to make sure I don't look like anyone else."' She has gone out of her way to remain true to her word ever since.

'Growing up in Anaheim, California, I always made my own clothes,' she said. 'In the beginning I'd go to thrift stores, or places like The Wet Seal and Contempo Casuals, and try to find something weird. Then I'd take it home and remake it. I had a sewing machine in my room – it was the danger zone. It was, like, pins and needles everywhere.' When her brother dragged her into his band, her skill with a needle would come in handy creating merchandise for them. 'My girlfriend and I went to every single Sears and JC Penney's and bought out every single child's extra-large T-shirt and tank top. We printed pink No Doubt logos on them and sold them at our concerts.' She would also buy the baggy trousers from the boys' section of the charity shops 'because I never really liked my legs or butt' – although it was also a fitting tribute to one her favourite ska band's most successful songs.

> I'd go to thrift stores, and try to find something weird. Then I'd take it home and remake it.

That was more or less Gwen's life for 18 years. She had very few ambitions, and did not know where her life would lead her. She was a very passive child, happy to go anywhere that Eric pushed her but with no real aspirations of her own. At this stage, her greatest hopes were for routine suburban life as a wife and mother. That would all change when Madness struck.

Madness

As a child, Gwen's tastes in music were pretty tame; she cites Julie Andrews and Kermit the Frog as two of her earliest influences. Her brother, Eric, took it upon himself to educate her. It was the early eighties, and Second Wave Ska was gaining a foothold in the country.

Ska music, an early precursor to reggae, began in Jamaica in the 1960s. It combined elements of mento (Jamaican folk music) and calypso (which has roots in the Afro-Caribbean slave trade), along with American Jazz and R&B music. One theory is that the word 'ska' is simply a contraction of 'speed calypso'. Whatever its origins, ska grew in popularity and came to be influenced by other forms of music, including rock, soul, and the emerging punk phenomenon of the 1970s.

Madness were a British ska group who became extremely well-known in the early 1980s – one of the UK's most popular bands, with hits like 'Baggy Trousers' and 'House of Fun'. Combining ska with more traditional pop, their 'nutty sound' did not receive such acclaim in the US, although there was a cult following and they were often to be seen on early MTV. The Nutty Boys, as they came to be known, were one of the staples of Eric Stefani's musical diet, and Gwen grew familiar with their sound as he bashed out their hits on the family piano. More talented at the keyboard than he was as a vocalist, it fell to Gwen to sing along with him. Come 1986, Eric's reverence for Madness would inspire him to form a band in its image.

No Doubt

The band formed in the summer of 1986, while Gwen was still in high school. The driving force behind this idea was John Spence, a charismatic, athletic guy who met Eric when they were both working at the local Dairy Queen (Gwen also found her first job here, scrubbing the floors). They became best friends when Spence transferred schools to Loara High, like Eric. Their shared love of Madness and ska music led them to try their hand at it themselves, with John on lead vocals and Eric on keyboard. Casting around for a name, they seriously considered Apple Core, after a catchphrase from an old Warner Bros cartoon (often spoken by Bugs Bunny). Eric was a keen cartoonist, and often tormented Gwen by drawing caricatures of her.

In the end, though, they named the band No Doubt, after one of Spence's own favourite catchphrases. Eric told Gwen she would sing backing vocals, to which she naturally agreed. At the time in California, she wasn't used to seeing women singing on stage. If they were, they were almost invariably backing singers in punk bands – women of whom Gwen was in awe. 'I'd be mesmerised by them when they'd sing their few little words, I'd stare at them the whole set and want to try to do it like that.'

> **'I'd be mesmerised by them when they'd sing their few little words, I'd stare at them the whole set and want to try to do it like that.'**

A number of other musicians joined them for their early gigs, and many others would come and go in the band's early days as they evolved their sound and developed into the tight-knit line-up that began to pack in audiences the early 90s. Most of these early band members were friends or relatives of Eric and John. Even among what were often no more than enthusiastic amateurs, Gwen didn't know what she was doing there. 'I had no idea I could sing,' she said.

Besides, there was already a lead singer, and she couldn't hope to match Spence's charisma on stage. While she moved awkwardly and sang her backing part, Spence would wow the crowd with his signature back flips. Inspired by the punk band Bad Brains, he would scream his lyrics into the microphone and do everything he could to whip his audience into a frenzy.

All that would change : in later years, most of the band's publicity would focus on Gwen, often to the chagrin of the others. But to begin with, she felt like a fish out of water; it seemed she was just a spare part with little of her own to bring to the group. No Doubt – at that point an eight-piece band including a brass section – played their first gig at a party on New Year's Eve, 1986. It would be the first of many.

As time went on, Gwen found a new attraction to being in the band. It came in the form of Tony Kanal (sounds like 'canal'), a junior at high school and, at 16, a year younger than Gwen. Tony was of East Indian descent, but had been born in Kingsbury, England, and moved to California at the age of 11.

At that stage, the newly-formed No Doubt were moving slowly, playing poorly-organised and raucous party gigs here and there. Then, in March 1987, they gained their first 'proper' performance, at Fender's Ballroom in Long Beach, California. Fourteen bands were playing that night, with The Untouchables headlining and No Doubt scheduled second. Tony was one of the hundreds of people in the audience. Up to that point, Tony's musical influences had run to Prince and hip-hop, and his experience of bands had been playing the saxophone and bass guitar for the Anaheim High School Jazz Band. When he saw No Doubt performing, he was an instant convert to ska, and decided he wanted a piece of the action.

In the early days, the band's bassist was Chris Leal, a friend of Eric Stefani's. Unfortunately, Chris wasn't much good at playing live performances and had to be replaced. When Tony found out the band were looking to find someone new, he got in touch and arranged an audition. He duly turned up at the Stefani's house a few weeks later to try out. With long hair, Mexican sandals and oversize trousers, he cut a strange-looking figure. Still, Eric and John recognised his talent after only two songs, and brought him on board immediately. He would prove one of the mainstays of the band in the years to come.

Tony was an absolute perfectionist, and his attention to detail was the stuff of legend. He later became No Doubt's unofficial manager, competently taking care of the band's administration. Whilst his care and persistence paid off when it came to his music, the others would occasionally find it frustrating. Accordingly, they nicknamed him 'Kanal', pronounced to rhyme with 'anal'. Tom Dumont, who later became their guitarist, tells a brief anecdote to illustrate this aspect of his personality. One day, Tony was sending out mail for the band's promotion, and complained to Tom that the stamps weren't sticking. 'Show me what you're doing,' Tom said. Tony took another stamp and licked it. Then he licked it again, and again. 'That was the perfect description of his personality,' Tom remembers. 'He wanted to make it stick so bad, all the glue came off.'

Excuse Me, Mister

Tony's attention to detail and musical skills were a great asset to the band. More than that, Gwen was instantly smitten with the East-Indian bassist. She still felt out of her depth, but suddenly there was a really good reason to stick around in No Doubt.

She had known it as soon as she had seen him getting out of his car. (His odd appearance hadn't bothered her; Gwen is a great fan of being yourself. 'Don't shave, don't shower, don't care. Be really stinky and wear the same clothes every day. I think what makes a man sexy is not being self-aware. That's what's really cute to me,' she says, when asked what she finds attractive in a man.) It took Tony a little while longer to catch on. One of the problems was that Gwen was Eric's little sister, and the only girl in the band. The guys were all close friends, and there was an understanding that Gwen was off-limits; it was like they were family. 'It was pretty much an unspoken rule that nobody dates Gwen,' Tony told VH-1's Behind The Music. 'You know, you had her older brother in the band and he was real protective. It was almost like a bunch of brothers and our sister.' The prognosis did not appear good, but Gwen was not about to be deterred.

It only took a couple months before she coaxed him round to her point of view. The band were still in their early days, getting gigs wherever they could. In June of 1987, they played at a party. Thanks to the host's provision of a keg of beer, the whole band got drunk and Gwen managed to convince Tony to take a walk with her. When she tried to kiss him, he recoiled in terror.

'No! The band! The band!' was all he could think. Eventually, Gwen's considerable charms and persistence won him over, and he gave in. He didn't know what he was letting himself in for. 'He thought it was a one-night kiss,' Gwen said. She had other plans. 'I was, like, in love.'

There is no doubt who wore the trousers in getting this relationship off the ground. 'Basically, I forced Tony to make out with me. This was 1987, we had been in the band only for a few months together,' she told *SPIN* magazine. 'He didn't even like me and I made him kiss me. Then I forced him to go out with me for seven years.' Having browbeaten him into submitting, she realised that she didn't even know what nationality her new boyfriend was. 'Chinese,' was the answer when she asked.

As far as personalities went, they were chalk and cheese. Tony's ultra-carefulness was a far cry from Gwen's carefree daze. 'Tony took care of everyone and he was on top of all the business,' she told *Blender* magazine. 'Nothing went wrong – no stone unturned, every corner cleaned. The opposite of me. I'm a mess!' Fearful of reprisals, Tony and Gwen kept their relationship to themselves. Tony, in particular, was fanatically secretive, petrified that it might cause rifts in the band. 'Oh, boy,' he remembered to *Rolling Stone* magazine in 1997. 'It was a secret of immense proportions.'

The magnitude of the deception was painfully clear to him, and became more so when the others gradually started to catch on. They didn't want to say anything in front of Gwen, and waited for their moment. It came four months after Tony started going out with Gwen, at a Halloween party. He had decided to come as a girl, complete with dress and makeup. He arrived a little before Gwen, and the rest of the band delivered their warning. 'If we find out you're going out with Gwen, you're dead,' they told him. Tony vigorously denied all knowledge of the affair – unsurprising, given that he had just been delivered a death threat – but later in the evening the band found him sitting on the pavement outside the house, his mascara running with the tears.

Tony was Gwen's first boyfriend, and his influence cannot be underestimated – on Gwen and for the subsequent history and success of No Doubt, and also her more recent solo career. Their relationship lasted for seven years, through the band's rise to fame and through the difficult times when nothing seemed to be going right for them. Once Gwen realised that she could write songs as well as just sing them, the subject of their romance and its ups and downs

began to permeate their lyrics, too. She even started wearing a bindi, the jewel or coloured dot worn on the forehead by many Indian women. 'We used to go to these Indian parties and I saw his mum wearing one,' Gwen recalls. 'I was just into anything that sparkles. I started wearing it and couldn't stop.' Whilst her fashion was, and remains, unrestrainedly eclectic and eccentric, she did not take on any of her boyfriend's family's religious customs, remaining resolutely true to her Catholic upbringing. When asked about her interest in the Hindu faith or the significance of her 'third eye', the most profound thing Gwen usually came up with was, 'No, that's how I communicate with my home planet.'

If Tony's mother found that offensive, it is hard to say exactly how Gwen's parents must have reacted to her new relationship. Patti claims that Gwen was always a daddy's girl, and even today, with Gwen in her mid-30s, Dennis isn't entirely happy with his daughter's status as a worldwide sex symbol. There must have been tensions between her parents' values and her own, not least in her father's desire to shelter her from corrupting influences. No doubt due to her strict Catholic upbringing, she is extremely reticent in talking about just how far and how fast they took their romance. When asked by The Face in 1997 if Kanal was her first sexual experience, she replied indignantly, 'I would never tell you that! Are you crazy? I would never tell anyone that. I have pretty strong feelings about that. If any girls were to ask me what my advice would be, completely wait as long as possible, wait till you're married.' Such sentiment is a far cry from most rock stars' lifestyle choices, but it seems that Gwen did not entirely practice what she preached. 'It's different when you get older and you have a boyfriend,' she hinted to The Face in 1997. 'Like, I'm 27. It's such a blessing that God gave us, we should be able to respect it.'

My advice would be, completely wait as long as possible, wait till you're married.

For a woman famed the world over for her provocative outfits and dancing, Gwen is remarkably coy about the subject in real life, often simply choosing not to talk about it altogether. That part of the interview ended abruptly, 'I'm not going to talk about that stuff any more.' When SPIN questioned her on the subject, the answer was the same: 'Please don't ask those kinds of questions.' Pushing the issue further, citing that its readers looked up to her and wanted to know her opinions as justification, Gwen conceded, 'All I'd say is avoid having sex with anyone until you get married. It just brings too many complications.'

Patti and Dennis numbered amongst the many complications. In general, her relationship with her parents was very good. Still, they found more than one reason for concern in their daughter's behaviour when she joined No Doubt, and it shocked them to see her occasionally compromising their morals. Swearing was another thing that they intensely disliked and vigorously disagreed on at times. 'Just a Girl' was the band's first big hit, a song about female liberation and Gwen's feelings of being held back because she was a woman. On one occasion the band were playing in Costa Mesa, California, and Gwen was driving down there with her mother. Patti had asked her not to swear on stage, not least because she had invited some relatives to the concert and did not want them to hear her daughter say that. Gwen agreed, principally to placate her mother.

When she got there and started singing, it struck her that this kind of compromise was exactly what the song was about: giving in and doing what her mother wanted for no other reason than that she was a girl and that other people would think it inappropriate. In an unplanned outburst, she vented her frustration by screaming at the crowd, 'Fuck you, I'm a girl. Fuck you, I'm a girl.' It became a kind of unofficial anthem for No Doubt, but Patti was furious. She refused to speak to Gwen for a week, even when she left to go on tour. Gwen was 24 at the time. 'I know it's really common for young people, but I hated to see her accept it,' said Patti later.

That was a few years in the future though, when Gwen had taken control of her life and started to speak for herself. In the meantime, she was happy to tag along and let others decide where the future lay. She and Tony would eventually manage to patch things up with the rest of the group, including Eric, who wasn't too thrilled about anyone dating his sister, let alone a band member. And that, for Gwen, was as much as she had ever wanted out of life. 'I remember being this 17 year-old girl, in love and really excited about my future with the boy that I thought was going to be my husband and we'd have babies, and that was my passion,' she remembers of her early days in No Doubt. 'At first, my brother did all the song writing and I was just doing what everyone told me. I was completely passive with no goals. I was in love with Tony and just happy to be in the band.' Soon afterwards, however, they would all be shocked by a much greater concern, a tragedy that shook them from their happy-go-lucky approach to life and threatened to tear the band apart altogether.

The Darkest Day of the Year

John Spence was No Doubt's front man, the one to guide the band through their first year of existence. He was a likeable, fun-loving guy who cared more about putting on a great performance than for the technicalities of good music. Howling his lyrics punk-style into the microphone and back-flipping into the crowd, audiences loved him and a large part of No Doubt's early success was due to his appeal. Another of his trademarks was a hat he wore, affectionately known as his 'fuzzy furry'. 'I think they were really bicycle seat covers that had not been sewn shut on the top. He got them at his work,' a friend recalled.

Although he could bring the house down at their gigs, off the stage there was something very wrong. None of the other band members realised it, but John was desperately unhappy. Even now, his friends are not sure what was going on. The band was doing well, moving slowly but surely upwards, gaining popularity around their home town. They were becoming well known in Southern California's under-ground music scene, gaining bigger and better venues to play at. Shortly after Christmas of

JOHN SPENCE

1987, a year after their first gig, they were due to play at the Roxy in Hollywood, their best offer yet.

It is unclear whether John's depression had anything to do with his band, or was personal. If it was the band, perhaps Eric Stefani's thoughts came closest. 'I wish I could have done something,' he told *Behind the Music*. 'I think a lot of it might have had to do with the pressure.' On December 21st, 1987, the remaining members of No Doubt were stunned to hear that their friend and founder John Spence had driven to a parking lot in Anaheim, where he shot himself in the head. He was 18 years old when he died. The group were utterly devastated. Later, Gwen would offer some of her own thoughts on their leader's decision. 'He had a lot of problems. He had a huge stage presence but he couldn't sing,' she told *The Face* in 1997. It seems that, in some respect, she and the other band members blame themselves for what happened. 'It's really sad when you look back – it's like fuck, if we'd just let him sing...'

Was that really the reason? It seems unlikely that John really killed himself because No Doubt told him that his singing voice wasn't up to scratch. Perhaps it was a minor factor, but his depression was very deep-rooted to begin with. 'There were some problems there,' Gwen told *SPIN*. 'He was kind of in and out of high school. His mom kept taking him out of school. He wasn't really in with a bad crowd, but his mom was really paranoid about it. For all the years I knew the guy, I only went to his house one time, but compared to my family, The Brady Bunch family, church every Sunday – it was different.' Whatever the root causes, the suicide of their front man nearly blew the band apart. 'When you're that age and you don't even know the person is having problems, it comes as a complete shock,' she told *Details* magazine.

Tony remembers getting the phone call from Eric Stefani, back in December of 1987. 'He just said, "Come over right away." I got there and he said, "John's dead."' Tony says the same as Gwen. 'None of us were prepared for that, none of us could see that coming. It just kinda happened, it just changed everything.' It was a rude awakening for Gwen and the others, and a formative experience for them all. 'When your friend dies like that and it's so unexpected it's very traumatic. I think it taught us all a big lesson in how much one person can influence so many different people,' said Gwen. 'He was in a lot of pain. He was a very important part of the band and it still haunts us.' As planned, No Doubt played the Roxy gig, now as a tribute to their fallen founder. Days later, they decided that they couldn't go on without Spence, and the band split up.

New Beginnings

After the tragedy of John's suicide, it took some time for the dust to settle. When they had all gained some perspective on matters, they decided that going their separate ways was not what John would have wanted. They reformed, the name 'No Doubt' now a monument to Spence's memory. The unpublished song Dear John, a tribute to the sadness they felt at losing their founder, also dates from these days.

Having taken the decision to reform, some changes had to be made. Gwen was not happy taking on the responsibility of lead vocalist, and so Alan Meade, formerly a trumpet player in the group, switched to take John's place.

Within a few months, however, he too had to leave. After he got his girlfriend pregnant, he decided that family responsibilities were more important than his place in the band. This time, Eric Stefani managed to talk Gwen into the job. 'She tends to be shy by nature,' said former band member, Eric Carpenter, a sax player who left to study journalism. 'It took a lot of convincing to get her to the lead singer position.' Gwen was unhappy about being centre stage, but agreed to give it a shot. She has been their leading lady ever since.

In the aftermath of Spence's death, No Doubt gradually pulled themselves together and streamlined their group. Aside from Gwen, Eric and Tony, they added a new guitarist, Tom Dumont. Tom was a heavy-metal fan who played guitar in his sister's group, Rising. When he happened to look in on one of No Doubt's rehearsals in the spring of 1988, he was another instant convert to ska. The metal scene in California wasn't up to much anyway, so he left Rising and asked to join them, instead. Tom remembers how he pulled his long hair into a ponytail 'to try and hide my metal thing'. He became the fourth long-term member of the band. Still, his background as a metal fan gave the group's performances a heavier sound. His influences included Black Sabbath, Judas Priest and Kiss, and that edge came through for No Doubt.

The next year, drummer Chris Webb decided to quit the band, and Adrian Young joined the line-up in his place. He had been a fan for years, and had once spoken to Gwen when he called the number on the back of the tapes they sold at concerts. Rolling Stone writes how it wasn't just about the music; he had once visited the store where Gwen worked, hoping to meet her. Having heard that she and Tony were on a break from their relationship, he thought he might be in with a chance. He never plucked up the courage to ask: before long she was back with Tony and it was too late. Still, Adrian wanted to join No Doubt so much that he even lied about how much experience he had. When they heard him audition and he told them how many years he had been playing the drums, they took him on. Gwen remembers bringing him on board. 'Adrian practiced really hard with our tapes. He lied to us and said he'd been playing since he was in Jr. High and it actually hadn't even been a year. We picked him, then found but out and it was too late, so he played catch up with the rest of us.'

Those were the beginnings of No Doubt's distinctive sound: a background in their mutual appreciation of British ska, with vestiges of Spence's punk, Tony Kanal's Prince and hip-hop, Tom's metal, and Adrian's rock leanings. Eric

Stefani was now the driving force behind the band. 'Kinda like the Dad,' remembers Gwen. 'Eric was the one who was born knowing how to write songs, he was the leader and had all the creative vision for the longest time in the early days.' Ska was still an under-represented music style in the States, and they were keen to make the most of every opportunity. Accordingly, they took up all the offers they could. 'For years we were an underground cult band,' Gwen told the Daily Record a decade later, when No Doubt's success had been cemented by several albums and numerous world tours. 'We sat in the garage and made fun of every other band that was on MTV. Our first shows were very intense.'

In the late 1980s, their energy and enthusiasm gained them a loyal following of first hundreds and then thousands of fans. This was strange for Gwen, who had never expected to find herself as the lead singer of a famous band. All of this had just 'happened to her,' apparently without much intent of her own. At heart, she was still the shy girl whom Eric had coaxed into singing along to his piano recitals, and then browbeaten into joining his band. She had just gone along for the ride, and now she found that they were going further than she had ever expected. Despite her surprise, she said, 'I'd always felt famous, at least in Anaheim.' That kind of exposure she could deal with, but it wouldn't be long before things would get pretty strange for her. 'When it went worldwide, well, that was just plain weird. I'm a very private person, and so getting used to that kind of limelight was never going to be easy.'

Greener Pastures

1991 saw Gwen and No Doubt's first real step towards stardom. At the time, a lot of the songs they played were simply cover versions of UK ska hits. The band had gained some popularity around California, but it was still a small-scale operation; Tony was still acting as their manager, and their main sources of publicity were the adverts he sent out to an ever-growing mailing list. They were getting to play at a lot of parties and clubs through these, but there were few bookings for large gigs where they could made a splash. Another problem was they weren't getting any airtime: they were desperate to be played on a popular Los Angeles radio station called KROQ, which as its name suggests played hardcore rock'n'roll. When they tried to get on their playlist, it was made clear to the band they station didn't have airtime for what it saw as a minority-interest, Jamaican-music fusion band.

The upshot of all this was No Doubt were not making enough money from their music to give up their part-time jobs. Gwen and Tony both worked as salespeople at the Broadway Department Store; Tom ran a small business renting out music equipment; Adrian was a waiter at a local steak house; Eric, however, had found a way to capitalise on his love of cartoons and in 1989 had found work as an animator on The Simpsons. Gwen was studying Art at California State University, Tom was majoring in music, and Tony and Adrian in psychology. Any gigs they played had to be fitted in around these jobs and their study commitments.

Finally, after years of playing parties and minor venues, they gained some recognition from the industry. It took a Brit – a man called Tony Ferguson – to recognise their potential. Ferguson had worked for the eccentric Stiff record company (slogans include 'If it ain't Stiff it ain't worth a f**k') who had signed the great Madness, and was just the person to realise how far a ska act like No Doubt could go. He took some of the newly-formed Interscope label's high-flyers with him to see the band in action.

When they saw the following this underground band had attracted and heard them playing, Interscope promptly sat up and offered them a recording contract in August of 1991. At that point, Interscope were a small label that concentrated on alternative music, though in time they would grow into a thriving international presence. It was an exciting time for Gwen and her band-mates, although recording their album, given all their other commitments, proved a labour of devotion. Between October and December 1991, the band drove countless times to L.A. to record their debut album, eponymously titled *No Doubt*. It consisted of 14 songs, including some of Eric Stefani's material from the band's early days.

By now they were a professional outfit, which did not look a gift horse in the mouth: they devoted themselves to delivering their best. The album owed a great deal to 80s pop as well as their ska roots with Eric's synth keyboard and their brass section both pronounced features, not to mention Tony's energetic bass playing. If Gwen was still shy about performing, it didn't show: her strong and confident vocals gave Interscope boss Jimmy Iovine high hopes that he would see her grow into an international star. Gwen remembers overhearing him telling someone, 'That girl will be a star in five years.' It turned out to be a prescient but overtimed prediction.

'It wasn't a scientific insight or anything,' Iovine later told *SPIN* magazine. 'They were young. I knew they needed a lot of work. Five years was just a figure...I can't believe she remembers that.' Given that Iovine had had a hand in launching the careers of the likes of John Lennon, as a solo artist, and Bruce Springsteen, no wonder Gwen put her faith in his word.

However, when *No Doubt* was released in March 1992, it bombed. At the time, the grunge phenomenon was working towards a peak, its angst-ridden lyrics, distorted guitar riffs and anti-fashion clothes (which were soon taken up by the fashion industry) appealing to teenagers the country over. In the light of this relatively short-lived but intense competition, the album sold only 30,000. It didn't help that the pop contribution alienated many of their potential ska listeners, either. Depressingly, KROQ still refused to play any of their songs. Adrian remembers a producer for the local station saying, 'It would take an act of God for this band to get on the radio.' A financial flop, Interscope could no longer back them, although Ferguson claimed that 'We never lost faith in the ability of Gwen Stefani to become a star.' He said this to *SPIN,* in 1996, after their third album had already made that a certainty.

With the record company withdrawing their support and refusing to fund either a tour or a second album, it was suck the lemon time. They buckled down and carried on regardless. They began a two-week tour of America's western states, headlining for bigger bands in 13 performances. A few months later, in an effort to boost publicity, they funded a video for 'Trapped in a Box', one of the No Doubt tracks, for $5,000. Unfortunately, MTV never even screened it.

The 'Bleak Period'

Following this setback, many bands would have consoled themselves with the thought that few enough came even this far, then returned to playing the rounds of parties and clubs for which they had achieved at least local success. No Doubt, though, realised how close they had been, and were not content to give up that easily. They decided to have a go at doing it themselves. 'We came back from our tour in '92 and built a studio in our garage which is directly across the street from Disneyland, where we could hear the Matterhorn and fireworks every night,' said Gwen. 'We just sat in there and demoed and demoed and kinda learned how to make a record.'

The choice to go it alone was a brave one. No Doubt had already had more than their fair share of difficulties and in different ways the next three years would prove just as tough They would learn a lot about making music, and a

ERIC STEFANI

lot about themselves, along the way. Gwen found these years particularly turbulent. She discovered that she was a capable songwriter – an empowering time in which she learnt that she did not have to remain a passenger all her life. At the same time, there were various heartaches, including the break-up of her long-term relationship with Tony Kanal.

There were tensions within the band which, although eventually resolved, took their toll on all of them. The ups and downs of Gwen's life inevitably came through into her song writing. Many of the songs on No Doubt's next big album, *Tragic Kingdom* (so called because that's what one of Tom's school teachers used to call the nearby Disney Land), bear the scars of those years of her self-discovery. Gwen and the rest of the band call these three years their 'Bleak Period'.

They began working on a new set of material, recording in their garage-studio and learning as they went along. Eric was still their guiding light as a songwriter, though all of No Doubt's different influences played a part in the final form of their music. They made sure that the band worked as a democracy. The songs from this period had a less polished sound, which owed more to punk than the lighter pop that had influenced their first attempt – and, to some fans, contaminated it.

Gwen was cruising along, happy in her relationship with Tony and content as the lead singer but while she putting material together, with no real backing from Interscope, she turned her hand to song writing. She found that she had more to give than the singing: it was excilerating to discover that she could express herself through writing her own material, rather than just singing the songs her brother had composed. Since childhood, Eric had been the talented one, who had made up lyrics and improvised music for the band, and had cajoled Gwen into singing them for him because that was one area in which he did not have any flair.

'There was three years writing in our garage until *Tragic Kingdom* came out. I learned how to write songs halfway through that record,' she remembered. 'That is when my life changed. I went from being this really passive girl to "Oh my God. This makes me feel so powerful when I write these words." It was such a turning point to find that I had a talent and I had something to contribute, somewhere.' It was a 'eureka' moment for her, both in terms of her position in the band and for herself as a person. 'Once I knew I could write, I blossomed. It was like, power. Suddenly you don't have to be dependent on anyone else for happiness because you've got this thing you can do.'

It is to this moment of self-discovery that Gwen can attribute the rest of her career. Without the confidence that song writing gave her, half of No Doubt's hits would simply never have existed. At the same time, though, it also had the direct result of beginning to change the dynamic of the band. It was disheartening for Eric, in particular, who was unimpressed with the direction things were taking. There were also tensions between him and Tony. All in all, it was a hard time. 'We were barely hanging on by a thread,' remembers Gwen of that Bleak Period. Despite her own rebirth as a songwriter, she said, 'We were ready to quit and save ourselves from becoming a bunch of losers.'

We were ready to quit and save ourselves from becoming a bunch of losers.

One of the hardest things was that Interscope had lost faith and all but given up interest in their contract. Having come so far in their early days, it was a massive disappointment. 'The biggest problem was we weren't able to put out music and it was like three years between records,' said Gwen. 'I remember the first year the band came together it seemed like so much had gotten done and the last three years it was like nothing happened.'

Their answer to this was to produce and sell *Beacon Street*, a collection of B-sides from the material that would eventually make the grade and end up on their next proper album. It was a stopgap measure, intended to give them confidence and renew commercial interest in the band. It was named after a street in Anaheim where several of No Doubt's members lived. The garage studio where they recorded most of the album was also there. 'It was one of the best things we ever did because we were able to take some songs that would have probably gotten lost and document them,' said Gwen.

Yet *Beacon Street* was produced at home and sold in local music shops and at their gigs. The initial press of 1000 CDs sold out and Trauma records, which was owned by Interscope, picked up the vibe. Gwen said, 'It was awesome because at the very end, when we were mixing our album, we hooked up with these guys from Trauma, which happens to be a subsidiary of Interscope.'

From being a 'loser band,' tempted to quit at any moment to avoid becoming a bunch of second-rate flops, their luck had turned in the space of weeks. 'It's unbelievable how fast it has changed,' said Gwen. 'We're just trying to take every day and just enjoy it because we know it could be gone at any second.'

Yet No Doubt were just about to hit the big time.

REISSUE OF
NO DOUBT'S
INDEPENDENT
1995
RELEASE

The Beacon Street Collection

TRAGIC KINGDOM

Their next album would be a raging success, but there were painful experiences along the way. As Gwen put it in 1995, 'We went through some really bad times in the past couple years. Our way of dealing with that is humour and I think that's really apparent in the record'. Tony said it the same way. 'Tragic Kingdom is a battleground,' he said. 'It was the outcome of three years of struggle.' The style and content of that album was born out of the pain and tensions of those years, and without them, there is no question that Tragic Kingdom would never have been the success it was.

Fans could identify with the material – much of it inspired by Gwen's own personal angst – precisely because of her honesty and openness in talking about her feelings. Gwen tends to wear her heart on her sleeve, especially when it comes to writing songs, and it often seems that her music is as much a form of therapy for her as it is entertainment for her listeners.

The first of these tragedies was that Gwen's brother, their leader and teacher since the death of Spence, decided to leave the band. The three years since their unsuccessful 'debut' had not been kind to them, and there had increasingly been arguments between the key members. Gwen's new status as singer-songwriter had begun to impinge on Eric's territory. He had always been an artistic guy – cartoons and music were his two great passions – and he found it hard to compromise. He had worked part-time as an animator on The Simpsons since 1989, and had come home every day to work on new music for the band. It was discouraging to find that his hard work was not paying off. Interscope, in an effort to hone their songs into something they could sell, sent in producer Matthew Wilder, to help them shape their work into more consumer-friendly form.

'That period was an educational period, because it was growing and learning to play by the rules of the record company,' Eric later said. What is clear is that he did not appreciate the outside influence, and the changes they had to make to their music to accommodate the label. Artistically, the group was taking a new direction, and he didn't like it.

They were moving away from ska, their first love, and the genre that had inspired Eric to form the band in the first place. In addition, there were growing tensions between Tony and Eric – No Doubt's leading lady's boyfriend and brother. It is possible that there had always been difficulties between them, ever since Eric had had suspicions of Tony's romantic interest in his sister. After Spence's death, Gwen and Tony had realised that there were more important things than their secret, and had confessed all to the others; whatever difficulties it had caused at the time were insignificant compared to John's suicide, but they simmered under the surface for years afterwards.

Tony and Eric had never seen eye-to-eye. This did not stretch to explicit hostilities; it was more that they were very different people, with very different attitudes to the band. Tony, the band's unofficial manager, was a careful businessman, who had the group's financial and practical interests at heart. Eric, the founder and leader, was an artist, who did not like to curb his creativity over such material concerns. The awkward truth is that No Doubt needed them both, and Gwen was stuck in the middle. Increasingly, Eric was being pushed out. Song writing and composing had, until recently, been his preserve. He had always encouraged the others to try their hand at it; now, however, it was starting to threaten his role in the band.

Gwen was the one starting to take a front seat. Eric was moving into the background.

The tables had begun to turn: Eric was in the same position that Gwen had been, years earlier, feeling like a spare part. Instead, Gwen was the one starting to take a front seat. Eric was moving into the background. 'I was trying too hard to put my personality, or my being, on this planet through the music,' he told Rolling Stone. 'And I didn't know how to express myself any other way. So when that was compromised, I was lost.' That loss put a significant strain on his relationship with Gwen, who did not know which way to turn. She was growing steadily more confident, more outspoken, and becoming more creative. Far from being the backing singer in a band full of big personalities, she was now becoming the personality of the band itself. Eric saw her transformation and was, at the same time, pleased for her and unhappy about its consequences for him. But she could not turn her back on this new version of herself. It was simply a case of the band not being big enough for the both of them.

Throughout 1994, Eric started to get more and more depressed. He began to skip rehearsals – a pointed gesture, since they were actually held at his house. Then, shortly after they released the *Beacon Street* collection, he quit altogether, leaving to pursue a full-time career as an animator on *The Simpsons*. One of the last things that Eric wrote for the band was called 'Bye Bye Birdie' – a song about a bird ready to leave the nest and fly away. It was a tribute to his time in the band and his sadness that it had to come to an end. The song was never recorded, and in September 1994 he said his own goodbyes.

Eric's departure was not the end of his involvement with No Doubt. The *Tragic Kingdom* album had been the result of years of work, much of it his. Gwen was of the opinion that he deserved as much credit for it as the rest of them. That included having his picture, along with the others, on the cover of the new CD. He was brought back in for a day of photographing, and Gwen remembers what an awkward experience that was. In almost every picture, Eric was on the margins of the group, standing behind the others in the background, or at the side, looking away from them. 'It was very weird,' Gwen said. 'It was horrible.' The strain on her was immense, and it seemed that her previously close relationship with her brother would be shattered forever. In the end, the two of them actually went through therapy – at their parents' request – in order to solve their differences.

I didn't want to lose my brother, you know, because everything that I am is because of him.

'I didn't want to lose my brother, you know,' she told *Rolling Stone*, 'because everything that I am is because of him.' That was one of the awkward things. Eric had set Gwen's career in motion, and she knew that she owed him her success. Still, when Eric left, there was a vacuum, and Gwen was always going to be the one to step up and fill it. 'When that whole thing happened and he left the band it was a huge, huge, disturbance – especially for me because I could never picture No Doubt without him. But I think in some ways it worked out good because a lot of creative space opened up and that's where I fit in.' There is no question that Eric quitting the band was another defining moment in her career.

With hindsight, Gwen was balanced in her opinions of her brother leaving them. She still felt that he was a big part of what they did, and his legacy

would always be evident in their music. 'Everybody asks, "Oh, doesn't he regret it now?" But it's not like that at all, not even close,' she claimed afterwards. 'He's just as excited as all of us, except he doesn't have to do all the work! I think he really is very proud.' She honestly believed he would be happier after he left, able to properly fulfil his creativity in a way that wasn't possible at the time. 'He is one of those people who are really satisfied sitting in his room playing his Casio keyboard and making it fun for himself. So it was monotonous to play the same things over and over and be on tour, it's just not what he's into. So he finished the record and decided to do his art full time, that's his true love – his art.'

'Bart. Bart was the whole reason I got involved. I relate to him,' was what Eric said for himself. He continued to work with *The Simpsons* for a while, but quit after No Doubt went international. After all, he was the talent behind some of their most famous music, including Gwen's power-ballad, . Following *Tragic Kingdom*'s launch, he would find himself inundated with song writing deals from music companies, allowing him to exercise his creativity in whatever way he chose.

Ex-Girlfriend

As if the loss of one of her role-models was not enough, Gwen also had to endure the loss of another man in her life. It happened within a few weeks of Eric leaving: a double-whammy that left her shocked and uncertain. This time, the parting was much more ambivalent. The process – and the pain – lasted a lot longer, and certainly played an even greater part in shaping her character and music, and therefore the success of both No Doubt and her later solo career.

Tony and Gwen had been an item since the earliest days of the band. Gwen had fallen for him the first time she saw him, and after a few months they had begun a relationship that – although stormy at times – had lasted as long as their ska group's seven-year history. Aside from the romance, they were best friends, and thanks to the band, they saw each other almost every day. When things finally hit the rocks, it was a very difficult and lengthy process for the two of them to extricate themselves from the other's life. Gwen is always clear that she was the prime mover in their relationship. She had been the one to pursue Tony, not the other way round.

'I forced Tony to go out with me,' she recalled. 'He wasn't even interested. When we made out that first night, I think he thought it was more of a one-night kiss. But then we started going out,' she noted. The long-term relationship wasn't what Tony had signed up for, and he started sweating as time went on and Gwen started hinting that things were getting serious. 'After the first year, I was going "When are we getting married?"'

That would be enough to make any 18-year-old man recoil. What he thought of as a bit of innocent fun had suddenly spiralled into a full-blown relationship, with the monster of commitment, marriage and children looming in the background. Gwen fully realises that she came on too strong. 'I think he started feeling really claustrophobic,' she said. It didn't help that he hadn't had any time to sow his wild oats; they had been together since high-school, and playing the field had never really been an option. 'He'd never had any kind of experience, as far as seeing other girls, since he was 16 years old.' All of this conspired to make Tony feel very, very uncomfortable. Seven years down the line, he finally bit the bullet, and broke it off with her. Gwen was devastated.

There was another factor involved. In the early days, one of the band's greatest concerns about their singer and bassist's relationship was that any friction between them might end up tearing the band apart. Now, that was suddenly a frightening reality. Aside from dealing with their own, personal pain, a major concern was how to prevent it damaging No Doubt. 'If we break up,' Gwen remembers thinking, 'how can we be in a band together? I was, "If you even see a girl in front of me, I will kill myself. How can we hang out each day, and I can't touch you?"' That, in fact, had been the glue in their romance for a while. 'That's why we stayed together for such a long time: because he was such a good friend to me that he could never hurt me.'

It was a very painful time for Gwen, knowing that their relationship was on borrowed time. Tony was doing everything he could to save her feelings, 'even though he was already killing me, just by me knowing he didn't want to be with me.'

One of the problems was that they were so close – and have remained so in the years since. It was very difficult to be cruel to be kind, and Tony left things a long time before he dropped the bombshell. By that stage, Gwen had a pretty good idea of what was going on, which hurt all the more.

'We knew things weren't right,' she told *The Face*, 'and I'd be like, "Obviously something's wrong and you don't want to be with me."' He would deny it to save her feelings. 'Tony didn't want to hurt me and we didn't want to break up because we had to be in the band together...I was so desperate for him.

It wasn't a clean break, either. They still saw each other all the time, and there was a huge shared history that made it very difficult to be around each other without falling into the roles they had been used to for the past seven years. She found herself in an impossible position: her feelings hadn't changed, and she couldn't get the space to move on. 'When we broke up, I still forced Tony to kiss me,' said Gwen. 'I was in denial. I might have lost the title of girlfriend, but in my eyes we were still together.' Tony, for his part, could have tried harder to enforce the break. He had the best of both worlds, though. Having been the one to break it off, he could still have her whenever he wanted. 'For, like, a year, he didn't have to come to my house when I demanded it. He didn't have to do anything. But when he felt like it, I was there. It was horrible.'

Now that Gwen is a superstar, Tony often gets asked why he dumped her. Most people think that he must be kicking himself for throwing away one of the planet's hottest singers. For a long time, his feelings were extremely mixed – especially after Gwen took up with Gavin Rossdale, to whom she is now married. So what went wrong? 'I don't expect anyone to understand exactly what happened,' Tony told *Rolling Stone* in 1997, three years after they split, 'and I really have no desire to justify and clarify. It's in the past, and that's it.'

It wasn't easy for him, either. Although he had been the one to tire of the relationship, it was just as confusing to part company with her (and even more so, when Gwen suddenly and decisively moved on, leaving him to contemplate any second thoughts he might be having). Just as things were beginning to brighten for No Doubt, this new problem threatened; for both of them, the future of the band was paramount. 'For quite a while it was difficult to face the other everyday, but we went through that because we didn't want to jeopardise the band,' he told *Circus* magazine in 1997. 'But three years are quite a while and as I said, we're over it now and we're friends.' One of Gwen's latest songs, Cool, talks about the transition and how they now have a solid friendship.

Tony obviously had real doubts about keeping the band together while things were that difficult between them. Gwen remembers one drastic solution he offered to ease the tension: Tony suggested that he leave No Doubt.

Gwen explained that it was because loved her so much, and presumably still put her happiness over his own. 'I would never let him,' she said – a smart move, for various reasons. When asked if she offered him the same deal, she merely laughed. 'Fuck, no!' she said.

Inspiration and Independence

Gwen had lost a brother and a boyfriend in short succession and the strain this placed on the rest of the band was considerable. But there was a bright silver lining to the pain. What she had lost in relationships, she made up in material.

This was the period in which Gwen moved from being the passive singer of No Doubt's early days to the confident composer and performer she is now famous for. The transition centred around that traumatic period, and it is not unfair to say that Gwen owes a large proportion of her success to it. One of the earliest and most important milestones along the way was a song on the new *Tragic Kingdom* album called 'Don't Speak'. In it, alternating between her little-girl-lost voice for the verses and a passionate, commanding tone for the chorus, Gwen pours out her heart about the aftermath of her failed relationship with Tony. 'You and me,/ we used to be together,/ everyday together, always./ I really feel/ that I'm losing my best friend,/ I can't believe/ this could be the end.' She then launches into a tirade against Tony, from which the song takes its name, forbidding him to talk about their painful split.

So much for music therapy. Apart from ventilating her feelings, the song was a smash hit. Her 'severe depression' over breaking-up with Tony gave her a chart-topper in the US, UK, Canada and Australia. In 1996, it was the most-played song to air on American radio – staying at the top of the Billboard Hot 100 Airplay for a then record-breaking 16 weeks. In the UK, it spent four weeks at the top of the charts, and sold over a million singles. Although the song wasn't particularly ska-based, it prompted a revival in the musical genre.

Suddenly – almost overnight – Gwen Stefani went from being a little-known American singer to an international icon. Although not everyone thought the song was genius. On the eve of it going No. 1 in the British charts, the UK rock magazine, *Kerrang!* wrote: 'Mere words cannot describe how abysmally gutless and sugar smothered it is... Much like an anteater with a punctured snout, "No Doubt" sucks badly.'

By that stage, however, the band was secure enough in their cult status to view such a laboured comparison as a compliment: Tony even suggested they had the review printed on the band's merch T-shirts.

The subject of their break-up, in all its resulting moods, inspired many of the songs on *Tragic Kingdom* – which has sold over 15 million copies worldwide. Gwen sings about her broken heart, about her difficulties accepting the situation, and about her anger at Tony for putting her in that position. The video for 'Don't Speak' is especially telling. It begins with a Garden-of-Eden scenario, in which a man picks an orange from a tree. It turns out to be rotten and writhing with maggots. Given that the man is played by Tony Kanal, it might be inferred that Gwen considered her own paradise in Orange County ruined by her former boyfriend. The rest of the video is based in a garage, the group playing as Gwen walks around singing her lyrics to them in turn. There are a couple of particularly poignant moments where she implores Tony, 'Don't tell me cos it hurts…' The video ends with Tony returning the orange to its tree.

How did Tony feel about all this? Not only was the success of 'No Doubt' directly and almost entirely reliant on aspects of his private life, but he was forced to collude in this by performing Gwen's lyrics about himself. As *SPIN* put it, 'like Fleetwood Mac and Abba before them, the group's success has both come at the expense of and has openly exploited the heartbreak of a central couple.' Insult was being added to injury on a daily basis. Not only that, but these were Gwen's songs that were being broadcast and sold to millions upon millions of listeners. 'Don't Speak' was an apt title in more than one way – Tony never had a chance to put his side of the story to the fans. 'It's fucking surreal,' he said. 'Think about being onstage playing these songs. I'm opening my personal life up to all these people.' He dealt with the bizarre exposure via a healthy mixture of denial and dissociation. 'I just can't get attached. I've got to separate myself from the music and lyrics.'

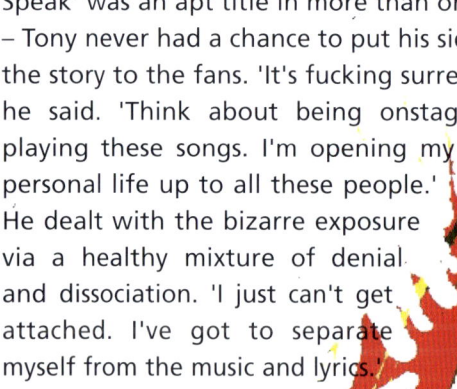

Eventually and inevitably, it started to wear a little thin. 'At first it didn't seem to get to Tony,' says Tom Dumont, No Doubt's guitarist. 'He was like, "I don't know, for some reason it doesn't bother me that all these songs are about me." Maybe he liked it. But now I think it's starting to bother him a little. Some guy wrote an article about us saying, "Why is Gwen so sad? What did Tony do to her to make her write all those lyrics."' Still, what could he do? Ask his band – and record company – to stop selling music?

Gwen generally manages to keep some perspective about all this in her interviews, and it is clear that she genuinely cares about Tony – whatever grief he gave her. She is equally frank about her own shortcomings. 'Everybody's like, "God, that guy is a jerk," which is not fair because he didn't have his lyrics to talk about me when I smothered him and he didn't have a life. It must be hard for him to take when people write "How could you leave Gwen, she's so great?" But they don't know me. They don't see my faults. They just see me however they want to see me. They think I have abs and I don't. I have fat.' Whether or not that is a conceit, she certainly admits putting Tony through the wringer. There was a period when she would call him and recite the lyrics of her new songs to him down the phone, berating him for his insensitivity under the cover story of asking for his artistic input. It all affected her more deeply than she thought. When the group returned from touring for *Tragic Kingdom*, she became clinically depressed as two years of roller-coaster emotions took their dues.

First Among Equals

However amicable the split eventually became, there must be a certain satisfaction in the irony that her subsequent fame was not only dependent on an extremely painful period in her life, but that the man who caused it has also been instrumental in putting her story out to the fans. No wonder Tony is loath to talk about it.

'Basically, it's a break-up song,' he said about 'Don't Speak'. 'But we didn't want the video to be about a normal break-up. So we thought: "What would be the saddest thing that could happen? The band splitting up?" So that's what the video's about.' Pushed by *Rolling Stone* about its relevance to him and Gwen, he admitted, 'Oh yeah, well the whole record is about that situation, but it's a good record, just lately everybody starts analysing the lyrics. It's all a while ago and we're friends now. We've done so much in the last year, and we've walked away from that. We're definitely friends now.'

Despite his understandable reticence, 'Don't Speak' did undoubtedly also serve to air some of the growing tensions within the band. It was a song that worked on more than one level. These issues can also be seen in the movie, as Gwen is repeatedly photographed and moved to the front, whilst the other members are asked to stand aside.

This happened for fairly obvious reasons. In a band of four, Gwen was the only female. She wrote many of their lyrics, and was also the only singer: the manifest voice of No Doubt. Publicity began to centre on her, and the record label increasingly used her looks and flair to market their music. As a result, the other three began to find themselves pushed into the background. It started before *Tragic Kingdom* came out, and has continued ever since – after all, which of the others has managed to cultivate a successful solo career? On the front of that album, Gwen stands provocatively, radiant and alluring in a bright red (and very short) dress, hand on hip and holding up a worm-eaten orange as a testimony of her own tragedy, showing off her blond hair, carmine lipstick and a broad smile. The others? Standing around in a field, very much in the background.

> It was a really honest video, but we had to sit on a couch together for a year and a half and answer the same questions every night and every interview.

This attitude began to spread beyond the purely commercial concerns of the record company. When interviewers spoke to 'the band', it tended to be Gwen they focused on – despite the fact that they had always stressed No Doubt was a democracy. When magazines printed articles and reviews, Gwen was the one singled out for special treatment. Although they all understood why it was going on, it caused a lot of friction between them. The 'Don't Speak' video helped air some of those grievances. 'It haunted us,' Gwen said. 'It was a really honest video, but we had to sit on a couch together for a year and a half and answer the same questions every night and every interview.'

The fact of the matter was that, whatever the effort and talent they all put in behind the scenes, Gwen was the show-stopper. She was the one who bared her soul in their lyrics. And, yes, she was the stunning 5'6" blonde with the bare midriff, skimpy outfit and fantastic body. Whatever the others tried, they just couldn't compete with that.

Still, it didn't do much for No Doubt's self-esteem to be regarded as a backing band for their lead singer. 'It's a lot different for Gwen because they are all looking at her,' Tony told *The Face*. 'Whereas we're getting her leftovers. So I'm not going to fool myself and say, "Yeah they're looking at me", when they're not. It's not me that drives all these people crazy when I walk out on stage. Oh great, here's the bass player, then here's Gwen!'

Tom was the one with the best perspective on all this, but even he was outspoken about how hard he found it at times. 'I understand it intellectually,' he said. 'But I just feel like I'm second-class, I'm shit compared to her. I feel I'm just a lesser person, I don't look as good, and I'm not as bitchin' as she is in everyone else's eyes. I think a certain part of me – the reason I wanted to be a rock star when I was a kid, I thought that would be a way for people to like me. And now that I get here, I'm not getting the payoff that I was always expecting.' Gwen herself was acutely aware of the imbalance in the way they were treated, and about the problems it was causing for them. 'Everybody just wants to focus on the girl,' she said. 'I think that's the one outside stress thing that has come into the band. We're getting over it. The others sit and bang on about me constantly now. Like, "On *MTV News*, Gwen broke her foot last night blah blah blah...and in less important news, Tom Dumont was found dead."'

It wasn't all roses for her, though. Being the sexy front chick of the band brought its own hazards. They had come an awfully long way since their early days, playing parties in whatever gaps they could find in the punk scene, but people still weren't ready for her. After the success of *Tragic Kingdom*, No Doubt toured for almost a year and, in1996, Gwen expressed her misgivings about some of their audiences' reactions:'The hardest thing on the last tour where we were opening – it wasn't our show, and there were lot of jocks and meathead type guys in the audience and every night I would have to deal with these guys being rude. It like got *Groundhog Day* after awhile. I started feeling like "what am I even doing here?" I thought maybe I should just go home,' she lamented to *The Vibe*.

Her appearance, intended to stun, had the desired effect; it just brought with it the risk that it would attract the wrong kind of attention. 'I feel like I was in a strip contest or something because of the way that they were treating me. Those types of things get kinda hard.'

Still, things had changed a lot over the years. No Doubt had been playing for a decade, when attitudes – particularly in California – were very different. 'The people who worked at the clubs just assumed I was a tagalong girlfriend or groupie. I'd get up on stage and the audience was just like, "Show me your tits!" I had nothing to show anyway,' she remembered ruefully. Perhaps these early frustrations were the origins of the hit single, 'Just a Girl'. 'I remember when we started playing as a garage band in Orange County, and you did not find girls in bands in 1987, at least in my little scene you didn't. If there were, they'd be the background singers…It's like they'd automatically assume that you were one of the band's girlfriends and ask to see your wrist bands and stuff like that. These days it's so much different and there are so many female artists, it's really nice to think that we're being taken seriously and people can enjoy the music. And that girls can go to shows and see other girls up there and be able to relate. I know when I was younger I didn't have that. I automatically had to be in love with the lead singer of the band you know.' Which was an interesting insight, as it turns out, because that was exactly what happened.

Hey Baby

Gwen and Tony were still wrestling with their feelings in the aftermath of their break-up in 1994. Two years after that unhappy event had thrown Gwen into a slough of despond, inspired half of *Tragic Kingdom*'s lyrics and prompted a world tour, she was still caught up in the difficulties that it created. Since they had become an international sensation, the band members were spending more time together than ever before. They were playing almost every night, usually headlining for bigger bands, and partying hard. There was no time out to gather her feelings and move on. That would all change in 1996 when she met Gavin Rossdale.

Gavin was the front man for the post-grunge band Bush, formed in 1992. Named after their former home in Shepherd's Bush, London, they were the first British band to make it big in America after Nirvana. Their story was one of almost meteoric success, graduating from playing minor gigs in London to huge arenas – stadia – in the States, seemingly overnight. Despite their popularity, many criticised that they were little more than a Nirvana tribute band, and that most of Gavin's appeal was as a poster-boy for teenage girls.

Gavin's past had been spent rather differently to Gwen's restrained and quiet upbringing (though he doesn't like people mentioning that he went to Westminster school, which the smarter rock hacks find they can't get their heads round). As a teenager, he had been a self-professed punk, coating his hair in egg white and putting glitter on his stomach. The latter may have had more or less to do with his friendship with Boy George. After his parents' divorce, he refused to speak to them and only remained on good terms with his sister. He fell into shoplifting and started to spend time in gay clubs – though he maintains this was only because of the quality of the music.

In his confessional 1995 autobiography, *Take It Like A Man*, George accused Gavin of having had a long-term affair with 80's pop transvestite, Marilyn. He described the Bush man as 'very flirtatious and ambitious'. He claimed, 'When I was writing *Take It Like A Man*, Bush were well on their way to rock stardom and he appeared at my house to persuade me not to include him and Marilyn.' But with a serialisation deal in the offing, George was not to be dissuaded. 'I agreed to leave some stuff out but I wasn't prepared to lie. I don't think Marilyn has ever really got over Gavin.'

Gavin was quick to set things straight, maintaining that the relationship was strictly Platonic. 'I'm not in any way homophobic, but I just hung around that whole scene. I grew up in the centre of London, and the best clubs were always the gay clubs...I wasn't dating Marilyn. We were, and still are, good friends. George thinks everyone is gay.' George admits that's 'true...but beside the point in his case.'

Lifestyle choices aside (Gwen has her fair share of same-sex admirers, incidentally), they had some common ground in that Gavin was also a singer-songwriter. Something else they shared was their record label, Interscope. Apart from that, and their shared status as pin-ups, the two of them seemed poles apart. 'I suppose that's why we're together,' explained Gavin. 'We have so many things in common, and so many things that are at the extreme ends.'

Gavin was a member of the infamously promiscuous Primrose Hill set (Jude Law, Kate Moss, Liam Gallagher), and his playboy lifestyle was a world away from Gwen's prim and proper upbringing. Nevertheless, when they first met around Christmas 1995, there was more than something in the air. In fact, it was to prove more accurate to say it was in the stars.

'Our record-company guys introduced us,' said Gwen. 'And I just remember looking up at him, because he is very tall, and going, "Wow". He looked so familiar to me; in his eyes, there was something about him. I said something like, "You've got gorgeous eyes," and I never say stuff like that. It was really cheesy, but it just came out. I don't know what he said to me right then, he was just being cool, but that night he told me I was gorgeous. I thought that was pretty great,' she remembers of their first, auspicious meeting.

Gavin remembers being stunned. 'I don't know what it was, something about her. She ruined my concentration.'

At the time, nothing happened. They both had their separate lives and careers, and although Gavin clearly was the type of person to go for a one-night stand Gwen clearly **When I get into somebody, man, watch out, because, like, I'm into it. I think about him the whole time.**

wasn't interested. It had never been her style, whatever the temptations of the rock-and-roll lifestyle. In fact, she has always shown admirable restraint as far as all the normal vices go, no doubt due to her strict upbringing. Besides, Tony was still, as far as she was concerned, recent history, and with the band's hectic schedule she had little opportunity – or inclination – to pursue a rebound romance.

'A lot of boys like me now,' she was forced to admit, after numerous tours and videos had made her an object of desire for millions. 'But it's not like I'm making out with people, you know, "Hey baby, come back to my room." I'm the kind of person who would way rather just spend time with my boyfriend watching a movie at home than going out to a party. That's the way I've always been. I'm not used to being on my own, to not having a boyfriend. When I get into somebody, man, watch out, because, like, I'm into it. I think about him the whole time.' Tony had found that out (to his cost), and Gavin was next in line.

Gwen wanted to be a strong, independent woman, particularly after Tony dumped her – as the lyrics of numerous No Doubt songs testify. 'I want to have a time when I don't need a boyfriend,' she said. Still, after a seven-year relationship, she wasn't used to being on her own and was hyper-conscious of what she really wanted. 'It's just nature to want someone. There's nothing better than that.' Fate and Interscope records contrived to change things when, in 1996, No Doubt was scheduled to open for Bush on tour.

Tom, Tony and Adrian were less than impressed by this turn of events. As a band with their roots in ska – whatever New Wave influences had brought them this far – their pairing with Bush grated on their sensibilities. Perhaps there was still just a hint of resentment over the miserable release of their first album, which the growing grunge movement had swallowed whole. 'The label was always talking about 'Gavin' and 'Bush',' Gwen remembers. 'We were just like, "Whatever. We are not going on tour with those guys; that's not what we are."' Gavin didn't want No Doubt opening for his band either.

'When I found out we were going on tour together I really had an anxiety about it,' Gwen told *The Face*. 'I thought I'd have to hide in my bunk.' The problem was simple. Tony was still very much a part of her life, and she felt bad about starting a romance with someone else. The whole uncertainty surrounded the feelings of a guy who had dumped her, over two years ago. 'Just the whole idea of Tony being there and there's this guy who might have a crush on me…' Something doesn't add up there, and fans might have been forgiven for wondering whether it was Gwen, not Tony, who had the issues. Either way, and for all her noble intentions, she gave in to Gavin's considerable charms. 'It was three days into the tour and we were in New Orleans, it was Mardi Gras and there was this huge party for our bands and we just had such a crush on each other even though we didn't really know each other,' she said. 'It had just built up since Christmas. We kissed that night.' Well, that as graphic as Gwen gets.

Still, even in the face of this moment of weakness, she maintained her misgivings. For the rest of the tour, and some time afterwards, the two of them were forced to profess that they were 'just good friends'. That was the official party line, to which Gwen stuck until 1997, when their relationship came out into the open. She couldn't even spend much time with him on tour, because she didn't want the rest of the band to disapprove. Perhaps Tony had begun to pick up on the fledgling romance, because he instantly took against Gavin. 'When we were on tour it was really hard – I couldn't hang out with Gavin because Gavin and Tony hate each other.'

After the tour ended, they started spending more time with each other, away from the ever-watchful eyes of the band and particularly her ex-boyfriend. Amidst growing rumour and almost daily phone-calls between them, Gwen still maintained the 'just friends' line. The problem? The same as last time: No Doubt had serious reservations about the pairing. When she decided to come

clean, the rest of the
band was livid.
'Everybody was against it,'
she said. 'It was a very crazy
time. There was already my
break-up with Tony, and we
were enjoying success for the
first time and having outside
things come in to our little band,
our little family... It was really
lonely, because I felt like nobody
wanted me to go out with him.
My ex-boyfriend and all of my,
like, brothers in the band were saying,
"You are not gonna go out with that
guy!"'

No Doubt had always been very protective of
Gwen, since the early days when she was a shy
teen playing at clubs and parties. At least one of
the reasons for their reluctance to allow their singer
to go out with Gavin was his rep as a real rock'n'roller.
'I had never been out with anyone else!' admitted Gwen
– unlike Gavin, whose bedpost is so notched it is in danger
of collapse. 'And other reasons. Everything you could think
up in your brain is probably true,' she confessed, rather
cryptically. In which case, speculation about Tony is well-
founded. Even after she had officially started her controversial
relationship with the Bushman, Gwen spoke about the pain it
must be causing him, and her own mixed feelings. 'It's hard for
Tony,' she said. 'I don't know what's going to happen when he
gets a girlfriend. Maybe I'll freak out. I want him to be in love. I
want him to be happy. I love him so much.'

The course of Gwen's true love – they eventually married – did not run smoothly,
presumably to some satisfaction from Tony and the others. For five years, it was an
on-off relationship that woke her up to a whole new range of heartaches (which, in
turn, proved inspiration for a vast number of new songs). Gavin remembers how
nervous she was on their first date – Gwen's first in a decade. 'I was talking to her, I
could see these red marks on her throat!' She was so anxious that she broke out in
hives. It got a little better after that, although it wasn't until 2002 that they decided
to make things permanent.

'HELLA GOOD'

No Doubt, meanwhile, were going from strength to strength. After the end of a hectic world tour (including Singapore, where swearing and provocative, semi-clothed dancing are illegal in public performances), they took a much-needed break. Early in 1998, back in their home county of California, they rented out a house in Hollywood Hills and started to put their minds towards new material. It was a point of departure from their earlier work, and even Gwen wasn't sure of which direction to take. 'We didn't know what kind of music we were going to write because we out grew our old style,' she said.

With a staggeringly successful tour behind them, and with the awards coming tumbling in, Gwen recalled what a difficult period in her life that was. Aside from her depression, she was trying to get a handle on who she really was. One side of her wanted to embrace the rock lifestyle and enjoy the attention they had won. But another side wanted to settle down, get married and have a family. There was a tension, as *Entertainment Weekly* once put it, between the Suzy Homemaker and the Suzi Quatro in her. 'It was definitely my least favourite two years of my life,' she said.

She was coming up to 30, and starting to ask all kinds of questions about where she was going. She'd spent over 12 years in No Doubt, climbing to the dizzy heights, and now there was a great sense of anticlimax. 'You start to feel like, this is me, this is what I am: all those years of blossoming, and now it's time to...perish.' It didn't help that she and Gavin were not having the happiest romance; there were numerous splits, and rumours flying about his involvement with other women. 'I've always been a happy-go-lucky, passive type who attached myself to one person and lived happily through them,' she remembered of that time. 'But I got to a point where I was going, oh my God, maybe this is what an adult feels like – and it sucks!' Needless to say, all of this was grist for the songwriter's mill, and Gwen's existential angst would surface in future recordings.

Tragic Kingdom had put Gwen – and the rest of No Doubt – under huge pressure. It had been a fabulous success and expectations were high for a repeat performance. But they all knew, being brutally realistic, that lightning

didn't strike twice, and that – even if they came up with some great material – they were unlikely to sell as many records as before. There was also, for all of them, a growing crisis of confidence: were they even supposed to be doing this anymore? Tom put it into words: 'I hate to say it, but in most cases, pop music is for young people. I think there's certainly exceptions – people who are truly talented who can write well into their 30s, 40s and 50s. Something usually happens, though – people lose it.' As time rolled on, and the work piled up but completion seemed further and further away, that feeling became acute.

There was no shortage of material, thanks to Gwen's personal life. (Asked what lyrical themes they dealt with this time around, Adrian was quick to answer: 'The last album was about Tony and this album's about Gavin!') The long-distance relationship wasn't easy, especially when she was spending so much time with No Doubt. 'There's definitely been some low points', she said about her romance with Gavin. 'It's really hard. It's probably the hardest thing I could choose to do, but any guy I go out with, it's going to be hard. I think it's hard to do more than one thing good, and right now, I'm doing the band. Any relationship I have is going to be suffering in some way. We make it work because we want to have a future together.'

One of their breaks prompted the song 'Ex-Girlfriend', and a hair-colour change to a dramatic shade of pink. 'That's what you do when you break up with someone,' she said, looking back on the troubled time. 'I saw a poster of some 50s girl with cotton-candy-beautiful hair.' In the event, it turned out to be less beautiful cotton candy than a vivid fuchsia. Nonetheless, she kept it for a year, and can be seen parading it on the 'Ex-Girlfriend' video (where the 'ex' in question looks suspiciously like Tony Kanal, rather than Gavin...). The hair in fact highlights how popular Gwen was becoming. It spawned thousands of teenage copies, and their own flamingo-coloured hair could be seen bobbing up and down at No Doubt concerts for years to come. One of the reasons that Gwen did not revert to her previous blonde for so long was to avoid disappointing these young 'Gwennabees', as the media dubbed them.

In retrospect, Gwen realises what a turbulent period that was for her. *Return of Saturn*, as their new album would be called – again at Gwen's suggestion – was taking forever to complete, and they were under considerable pressure to deliver. Its title was a reference to an astrological theory that touched a nerve in her.

Known about since ancient times, the Saturn Return links the orbital period of the planet – around 29½ years – to the time of introspection and self-evaluation that people often go through at that stage in their lives. Gwen was looking at turning 30, always an occasion to take stock and think about what life held. She'd been highly successful in her career, but her personal life was messier, and she was becoming ever more aware of that ticking body clock.

> I was 29, and I was like, "Fuck it, I'm going to dye my hair pink."

Having put dreams of kids and a family on hold for a decade, she was waking up to the fact that her time was running out. 'You can tell by my style that I was searching so hard. I was 29, and I was like, "Fuck it, I'm going to dye my hair pink." And I had braces, the one thing I bought when I got rich…' Looking back, she says, her pink hair was an outward expression of all that was going on inside. 'I look at it, and I go "uccch", but it so perfectly reflects exactly where I was, which was very unsure of myself. But if you read the lyrics of that record, they are some of the best I've written in my life!'

The depression really shone through in this one. Gwen had taken her blues seriously, looking for some miserable influences and immersing herself in their style. 'I got into Joni Mitchell and Sylvia Plath and reading and really trying to use words like they were colours.' It was a darker album, partly because of the content, partly because they were increasingly leaving behind the bouncy ska sounds of their earlier days, turning instead to rock, reggae and New Wave. Gwen was fairly realistic about the level of influence she had in the album: 'It's a selfish record in a way because the songs are largely about me – and my insecurities. I laid it all out there, and it feels good.' Tom had a slightly different assessment. 'It's probably a lot easier to have sex to this record than the last,' was his appraisal. Despite the levity, he and Adrian had voiced their misgivings about the direction things were taking. They wanted to play rock music; they weren't so sure about Gwen and Tony's predilection for the 'dear diary' lyrics any more.

Such lyrics did please the schoolgirl contingent, who now accounted for a large chunk of the band's audience – due in no small measure to Gwen's appeal to them as modern gal with an old-fashioned heart. At any No Doubt gig, hundreds of these 'Gwenitators' could be seen, dressed as they thought Gwen might, pink heads bouncing around in the audience.

Others, especially some rock critics, weren't so impressed with *Return* but Gwen was very pleased with the album and, more importantly, it did very well on release. Still, it couldn't touch the success that the earlier material had enjoyed; the Gwenitator demographic couldn't really relate to thinking about turning 30, marriage and ticking biological clocks. 'I think I wrote my best stuff on *Return of Saturn*, although I know it only sold four million – sorry and all that,' she commented later. The next album, *Rock Steady*, which followed shortly after *Return* in December 2001, was a lot more upbeat – a reflection of the direction Gwen's life was taking. It didn't hurt the sales figures, either; the CD was received rapturously by the fans and sold more than 250,000 copies in its first week.

Marry Me

September 14th, 2002 saw Gwen tie the knot with Gavin, after a nine-month engagement. He had proposed to her on New Year's Day and, despite having to ask him to repeat the question, she had agreed. Their relationship had not been a fairytale romance; every now and again in the previous six years, Gwen had been seen sporting bright and bizarre new coloured hair, one of her standard coping mechanisms when things went wrong and they took another break. Finally, though, here she was, her hair a very orthodox blonde. Her gown was slightly less conventional. In true Gwen style, she opted for something custom-made and unique, a pink and white Dior dress by John Galliano. 'She looked unbelievable,' one guest remembers – no doubt barely recognisable without a naked midriff. An antique lace shawl completed Gwen's dream outfit.

The church they chose was St. Paul's, Covent Garden (not the cathedral; for such major personalities, this was a very low-key and restrained affair). Band members from Bush and No Doubt were, of course, in attendance, though the crowd of fans outside was considerably larger than the 150-strong guest list. 'It really wasn't a big, glamorous, glitzy affair, says one of the guests. 'For two people with such high-profile lives, it was fantastically down-to-earth and ordinary.' As far as previous celebrity involvement went, the church has a very good pedigree. It is sometimes known as 'Actor's Church', due to the number of stars who have previously gone through its doors, and occasionally taken up residence. Vivian Leigh of *Gone with the Wind* is buried in the churchyard, and there are memorials to Gracie Fields and Boris Karloff inside.

Gwen turned up a whole hour late, at 6pm, in a blue 1970 Rolls Royce, and made her way through the 17th century churchyard into the building. Satisfying her desire for sparkly things, hundreds of stars had been hung on the trees. Inside, Gavin was waiting with Winston, his Puli (Hungarian sheepdog). Decorated for the occasion in a collar of flowers, Winston – who also appeared on the cover of Bush's Sixteen Stone album – would accompany Gavin down the aisle and would stay at his side for most of the ceremony. 'He didn't bark and was very well-behaved,' Gavin's security man Guy Johnson told *People Weekly*.

Although it was an Anglican service, Gwen included a nod to her Catholic background, carrying her grandmother's prayer book and a set of rosary beads as she walked up the aisle with her father, Dennis. There were certain elements of tradition that she wasn't prepared to forego, including the requirement that Gavin had asked Dennis's permission first. 'He was very gracious,' remembers Gavin.

As the two quietly said their vows to each other, Gwen was overcome and began to cry. She was not the only one. 'It was pretty emotive for both of them,' remembers Gavin's father. Galliano said the same. 'Gwen was visibly choked with emotion. She cried, he cried...and so did the dog!' (Perhaps this is true. Hungarian shepherds are said to sell their Pulik only to other shepherds, because they feel they are the only ones to understand the dogs' unique temperament. Puliks have sensitive souls). Once Winston had pulled himself together, the guests were ferried over to the reception in true London style by double-decker buses. The venue was an exclusive private club nearby called Home House, patronised by the likes of Madonna and others who can afford the £1000-plus yearly membership fees. The food, served in the courtyard garden outside, was another nod to Gwen's heritage – a seafood risotto and pasta meal, stretching over six courses. Partying afterwards finally wound down around 5am.

Two weeks later, the pair renewed their vows in a Catholic blessing on the other side of the Atlantic in Bel Air, California. This second ceremony was partly for the benefit of a number of their friends (including Ben Stiller, Brad Pitt, and Jennifer Aniston) who couldn't make it to London for the first one. And also because it gave her another opportunity to dress up. 'That dress,' she said, 'was the whole reason I had another wedding.' The guests met at the house of Jimmy Iovine, her boss at Interscope.

A Passion for Fashion

Following her wedding, separated by a brief honeymoon in Capri, a new phase opened in Gwen's life. Whereas her career had previously been tied to No Doubt, she decided it was time to strike out on her own in a few new directions (soon, it would seem like she had fingers in more pies than she had fingers). It was as if, suddenly having achieved security in her marriage, it left her free and gave her confidence to pursue other projects. Near the top of her list, along with the solo career she had been considering and discussing with Iovine, was her own fashion label.

Gwen had always been creative when it came to fashion. She had been brought up making her own clothes, and this enthusiasm found its way into her music career as she put together sometimes bizarre, sometimes over-the-top, but always eye-catching outfits for the stage. 'Music and fashion, it all comes from the same place of creativity,' she said. 'I don't see why any musician who has style or pays attention to style couldn't do it... It's an extension of my personality. I can't explain why I like it, it's just always been that way for me – like pizza.'

She was used to improvising, effortlessly throwing together eclectic elements and coming up with new creations to wow the crowds as she sang. That had been the way since she was 17 and first took to the limelight. 'I would buy old men's pyjama bottoms and peg them and wear my monkey boots and my tank tops,' she remembers. 'I was also really into Hollywood glamour: skinny eyebrows, lots of powder with red-black lips, and tons of mascara.'

She came up with the idea of starting her own line with her personal stylist, Andrea. The two of them were forever making new outfits for Gwen's tours, and selling designs was a natural progression from that. 'It's every girl's dream. We were going to do something really small and just sell our stuff at a few boutiques' was Gwen's initial plan. But whatever the line's humble origins, once others showed an interest and offered financial backing, it started to go places. 'I met this guy who said he wanted to do a clothing line with me and pay for everything. The best part was he said I could do whatever I wanted creatively. I was like, "Are you kidding, me? Okay!"' An already rich Gwen was instinctively showing solid business acumen – the rule in start-ups is never use your own money if you can avoid it.

The named her new clothing line LAMB. The inspiration for this hardly inspiring brand name was a dog she had had as a child. 'I had a dog for 16 years, and I called her Lamb because she was like the lamb in "Mary Had a Little Lamb" – she followed me everywhere I went. So then I thought Lamb would be a cool name for my clothing line, because it would be like my dog living on through my clothes.' In case sceptical backers needed more explanation, there was another, equally idiosyncratic, side to it : 'When we did the bags with Le Sportsac we decided that L should stand for Love, A for Angel, M for Music, and B for Baby. So there's a few meanings to it.' The main fashion line opened in Spring 2004, and was instantly a hit. Many big celebrity names have been seen toting her gear, including Halle Berry, Pamela Anderson, Nicky Hilton and Carmen Electra.

Gwen had been creating unique outfits since she was in her early teens, but doing it commercially somehow wasn't so easy. After the first success, she found herself in a creative dry period, in terms of both her music and her fashion. Inspiration was to come in the most unlikely of forms. During a trip to Japan, she stumbled across the Harajuku district of Tokyo, where teenagers gather to show off their unique creations. This 'subculture in a kaleidoscope of fashion', as Gwen put it, struck a lasting chord with her, as seen from subsequent song lyrics:

Harajuku Girls, you got the wicked style/
I like the way that you are, I am your biggest fan.

Harajuku was the muse behind a whole L.A.M.B. range, which included creations of Goth, lace and Japanese influence. It launched late in 2004, to coincide with her solo album, also called *L.A.M.B.* Her take on Japanese culture would make them both controversial and popular, securing her role as a fashion designer as well as a musician. She said, 'It's something that is going to be what I do to express myself creatively, that is a lot less draining than writing music or performing. I love that but I'm being realistic – I'm not going to be doing it the rest of my life.'

Fashion is her fallback. 'I think designing is something I could get really good at,' she claims. 'It comes naturally for me. I don't mean that I'm good at it right now, but I could be if people keep believing in me.'

Flying High

This period saw Gwen's success in yet a third arena. Having conquered the worlds of music and fashion, winning stellar successes along the way, she finally broke into the movie game after years of trying. *The Aviator* is a biopic about the life of eccentric billionaire and entrepreneur Howard Hughes, who rose to prominence as a film maker and aviation mover-and-shaker in the 1930s.

Gwen had made numerous TV appearances as herself in the past, including two episodes of the comedy show *Ellen* and one of *Dawson's Creek*. There was also a brief appearance as a guest star (with Tony Kanal) in the 2001 film *Zoolander*, in which No Doubt featured. But she had yet to appear in a film as an actress, something she had been desperate to try for years.

Her part as Jean Harlow in the Hughes biopic was only the briefest of cameos, but *The Aviator* was a Scorsese film, and that carried a lot of clout in any actor or actresse's CV. Quite apart from the director, she would be starring alongside some of Hollywood's stars: Leonardo DiCaprio played Howard Hughes, Cate Blanchett took the role of screen legend Katherine Hepburn, and Kate Beckinsale, Jude Law and Alec Baldwin also starred. She would be in very good company.

The story goes that Scorsese was having trouble casting the part of the 30's icon, Jean Harlow, who starred in some 36 films before her early death from kidney failure in 1937, at the age of only 26. In her brief but prolific career, Harlow became known as Hollywood's original blonde bombshell, predating and inspiring Marilyn Monroe's own career as a platinum-haired sex siren. Walking down Hollywood Boulevard one day, Scorsese happened to look up and see Gwen's picture on the side of a bus stop – a cover photo for *Teen Vogue* magazine.

'I was looking pretty fine and pretty blonde,' remembers Gwen, unselfconsciously. It is easy to see what captivated Scorsese about her: Gwen's fashion style radiated 30s glam. 'It's a perfect fit,' enthused celebrity makeup artist, Darrell Redleaf. 'Gwen's signature red lips, blonde bombshell hair and arched brows are old Hollywood.'

THE
AVIATO

Gwen, who had in fact expressed interest in the project some months earlier, was overjoyed to be considered for the part. 'It's bizarre,' she said. 'Growing up, my room was covered with posters of early Hollywood.' The influence that such actresses have had on Gwen and her fashion sense is obvious, and the part was a fitting tribute to that. Her excitement was only slightly diminished by the minimal screen time that Harlow's part required. 'He sent me the script and I spent 15 minutes looking for Jean Harlow because it's such a small part. I have two lines or something.'

Although her looks made her entirely apt for the role, she still had to get through the audition like everyone else. This – even for a veteran of a thousand stage performances – was a nerve-racking business. 'My stomach was on the floor,' she remembered of the experience. 'It's totally humiliating to walk in and have to try out. They know who you are, but it's a casting-call thing.' Success as a singer does not guarantee success as an actress, and she had precious little experience. 'It was torturous,' she said. 'I wasn't used to that pressure, competing against other girls and full-on actresses.'

Her concern was well-founded; Gwen had been auditioning for movies parts since 1999 without success. Her first attempt was for *Fight Club*, David Singer's adaptation of Chuck Palahniuk's cult novel. In the end, Helena Bonham-Carter got the part of Marla, Tyler Durden's beautiful but utterly dysfunctional girlfriend. More recently, she tried out for *Mr and Mrs Smith*, Doug Liman's action comedy. 'I did, like, 40 try-outs for that, I met with the director and everything, and I really wanted to do it.' That time, though, she lost out to Angelina Jolie. 'I was so upset about it, but it won't stop me,' she vowed. 'It won't. Movies are a challenge for me, and I do like a challenge.' (She wasn't the only disappointed one; it also paved the way for Brad Pitt to leave Jennifer Aniston for Angelina Jolie and keep celebrity gossip mags in column inches for months.)

Movies are a challenge for me, and I do like a challenge.

Along the way, there had been failures for *Girl, Interrupted*, *X-Men 2* and *Chicago*. For someone like Gwen, on top of her own game, being an also-ran was tough. Auditions, moreover, didn't agree with her. 'You are sitting in a room alongside all these other people who recognise you instantly, and that can be very awkward.' She desperately wanted to get into the movies, but she found it hard going from being a big fish in a small sea to being a small fish in an ocean. Especially when the part was so small.

The reason she persevered was the prospect of becoming a serious player in in the film industry. Even a two-line bit part in *The Aviator* did that because it was a Scorsese film. Filming began in July 2003, though it wasn't released in the UK until January 2005.

Gwen was entranced by her Hollywood debut: she saw a new door opening before her; she also felt a great affinity for Harlow's character. 'You can see that she inspired me. And it was really familiar, walking down the red carpet, so it wasn't really branching out.' Harlow's consummate style in the film can only have appealed to her own; decked out in white silk, fox-fur and orchids, Gwen looked and felt every bit the 30s icon. Her brief experience in *The Aviator* was a new departure in performing. 'Acting is a lot different than singing,' she told MTV. 'It's not as theatrical, it's a lot more subtle, and that's a lot harder. Simpler is usually harder.' The possibilities were intriguing, and the acting bug had bitten hard. 'So I would love to do more. I got my feet wet, but I would love to go swimming. *The Aviator* is a fantastic opportunity for me. It was an education and I want to keep learning.'

There was a parallel in Jean Harlow's and Gwen's situations. Howard Hughes had been the one to give Harlow her first major role, and Scorsese was the one to cast Gwen in her first part. After filming, she sent the director a bunch of flowers, with a note paraphrasing her one line in The Aviator: 'I would like to use this occasion to publicly thank Mr. Scorsese for the opportunity he gave me. Thank you.' Still, she is modest about her appearance in the blockbuster, and circumspect about future possibilities. 'I'm not a movie star,' she admitted. 'It's almost embarrassing talking about a movie that I'm only in for a couple of minutes. It's like, don't blink or you'll miss me. Leo and the rest are the stars and I'm just lucky enough to have a moment in it playing Jean Harlow – a real Hollywood legend.'

Her diversification from music and fashion onto the big screen came relatively late in life (despite the fact that, at 34, she was playing a 19-year-old). Still, it is a shift that is growing increasingly common: once a singer has achieved a certain measure of fame, moving into film seems to be the expected thing to do. This is achieved with varying degrees of success. Some, like Will Smith and Jennifer Lopez, have gone on to make it big in Hollywood. But for each one of those there are many others who fail dismally: it is a far more difficult bridge to cross than it seems. As casualties like Madonna (not to mention a slew of rappers) bear witness.

To some, this tendency to jump from musician to actor is anathema. Samuel L. Jackson, for example, recently turned down a part opposite the rapper 50 Cent in the film *Get Rich Or Die Trying*, on the grounds that Hollywood is always over-keen to offer such roles to successful musicians. Tom Waits (a musician who has made the transition well) compares the switch to 'going from bootlegging to watch repair.' It reduces an artist to the commercial value of their personality, rather than acknowledging any intrinsic ability that would merit a film career in its own right. The line between celebrity image (in all its forms, singing included) and legitimate talent is becoming increasingly blurred.

Gwen is not deterred. 'I would love to get to a position where I was known for my acting as much as my singing,' she said. 'I've been trying to do films for years, but it's hard to find the right roles.' Coincidentally, at roughly the same time that she was filming her brief debut in *The Aviator*, husband Gavin Rossdale (who was increasingly coming to be known as 'Mr. Gwen Stefani') was shooting a part as the demon Balthazar in comic-book adaptation *Constantine*. Either of their personality cults could propel them onto the big screen; whether or not the move would be a wise one – or will be cemented with further roles – has yet to be decided.

A Little Something Refreshing

2003 was also the year that No Doubt was invited to play at the 37th Super Bowl. Although the event didn't get the exposure it had the next year with Janet Jackson's 'wardrobe malfunction', Gwen loved the gig. The band played 'Just a Girl', alongside performances from Shania Twain and Sting – with whom Gwen actually later sang a duet. It was a cathartic moment for her.

She recalls how her father had been a marketing executive, and had worked with various bands – including The Police. As a child, Gwen had adored Sting, and Dennis had once been able to arrange a meeting with him. 'I actually met him for the first time when I was 16,' she told *Marie Claire*. 'My dad worked for Yamaha motorcycles, and he got me backstage after one of The Police's concerts. I was really fat and totally puberty-stricken, and my dad was like, "Ask him for his autograph." So I did, and he was really mean. But I still loved him.' Nonetheless when she performed with performed with him as an equal, she brought up the brush-off at the Super Bowl. 'I told him that story, and he was like, "Oh man, I was such a dick back then." But he's such a great guy.'

A BRAND NEW DAY

Although she was now married to Gavin, and on a hiatus from No Doubt, Tony Kanal still loomed large in Gwen's life. It must have been strange for Gavin, but Tony and Gwen were best friends and, musically, still very much partners. Gwen wanted to kick-start a solo career, and hoped to get Tony on board as a consultant. After their sell-out Rock Steady tour, she mooted the idea of a collaboration with him.

'Dude,' she remembers asking the bassist, 'wouldn't it be fun to do like a Club Nouveau record? Do a record just on the side. We're going to take a year off, why don't we do it? You could produce it, we could write songs like those songs.' Her intention? 'I definitely wanted to make a record that would get underneath the skin. I wanted to make a very good feeling, classic upbeat dance record that when you first heard it, it would be your guilty pleasure.' She was hoping to create something that would hark back to the 80s synth-pop of her youth.

So was put into motion the foundations of Gwen's very successful solo career. 'That's how the process started, and it snowballed.' It wasn't as simple as that, though . 'I thought it was going to be easy and fast because I'd work with a few people, do a few covers and I could just put a side record out, which people do all the time. After 17 years you try something different.' In actual fact, it was a torturous process that Gwen frequently found depressing and draining.

From the moment she'd suggested the idea, her record-label boss Iovine had been unreservedly enthusiastic about it. He knew that Gwen was gold-dust, and more than any of No Doubt would be able to cultivate a successful solo career. He backed her 100 percent. 'As soon as I told Jimmy Iovine that I wanted to do this record, it's been, like, his record,' she said. 'When someone believes in you more than you believe in yourself, you almost just want to do it to please them.'

The new album was to be called L.A.M.B., like her fashion line. Jimmy trusted Gwen's judgment and knew she would be a success. 'I would literally back her on anything,' he said. 'Her vision is that strong. I use her a lot in Interscope's

business, the way I would use Dr. Dre: "What do you think of this? What do you think of that?"' But Iovine also had ideas of his own: he wasn't just handing over the reins and letting her take charge.

Iovine pulled out all the stops. He knew he was onto a winner, and would spare no expense in putting her at the top. He brought a small army of consultants and musical genii on board, from all different genres. This would not be a ska-fest: it was a serious and deliberate attempt to appeal to as wide an audience as possible. As University Wire wrote, 'Gone are the highly personal and introspective lyrics that made No Doubt and its female lead so successful. In the place of substance, LAMB delivers '80s new wave and pop, with hints of swing and electronica. There is none of the familiar ska sound No Doubt is famous for.'

As a result, many previous fans would level the accusation (perhaps correctly) that she had sold out and abandoned her roots, but for every one of those she lost Iovine knew there would be another queuing up to hear this new Gwen.

Although this was a 'solo' move, in reality it was anything but: the album was a collaboration of big names, with Gwen as both the singer and attractive advertising for the package. Among the influences were Dr. Dre, the rapper and producer who launched the careers of Eminem and Snoop Dogg, André 3000, another successful rapper and hip-hop producer, Linda Perry of 4 Non Blondes, and a whole line-up of other big names, Tony Kanal among them. 'This record is a collaboration of a lot of great talents coming together and trying to make something that's classic,' she said of the project. 'Something that you want to listen to over and over. I want the album to be the record of "now" and to give people some kind of satisfaction and release.'

The various schedules of the different artists meant that Gwen effectively had to surrender control of 'her' project to others and allow herself to be pushed around at their say so.

'This is how crazy it was,' she remembers of the exhausting process. 'The record company called me and was like, "You've got to go work with Linda Perry. Now. She only has five days out of the whole year to work with you." And I'd just got off tour! I was tired, I was burned out, I'd just got married. I hadn't even seen my husband! But then I thought, OK, if I don't do this now... I want to do great things, and I know that I'm super-lucky.'

Given that Gwen's usual approach to writing songs was to wait for a personal crisis to come along and inspire her, working with such a group of people was a bruising experience. 'I was in the studio with all these great people, and I just felt naked before them, completely exposed. All these incredible ideas were flying around, but none of them were mine! I couldn't wait to get home to my husband every night and cry because I hated myself.' Song writing had been her identity in No Doubt; now she felt like she didn't have that anymore. She had worked with other musicians before; almost every song on Rock Steady had had a different producer. But this was different; frequently, it seemed like the project was being taken out of her hands completely. Producer Linda Perry, for example, worked a lot faster than she did.

Gwen remembers going off into another room of the house to try to work on some lyrics. When she came back, Linda would have finished the whole song. 'Dude, slow down. This is my record. Let me be a part of it,' Gwen would think to herself. On another occasion, she tried writing a song about a friend who had died. Before she even got going, Linda had finished the lyrics. It wasn't the fun project she had hoped. (Perry, for her part, found Gwen over-critical of herself. 'There was one day where she had a little insecurity breakdown. But I found it very endearing; I loved seeing her that insecure. You meet a lot of people who have half her talent and they think they're God's creative monster.')

Inspiration finally struck, this time in the form of Japanese street-fashion, the Harajuku girls who permeate this phase of her life – though Gwen simply calls it magic.

See, I've no idea how I write songs, no idea at all. It just happens, and afterwards I don't even recall how I did it.

'Magic saved the day! See, I've no idea how I write songs, no idea at all. It's not something that is in my control. It just happens, and afterwards I don't even recall how I did it. So there I was, flapping around and making a fool of myself, and magic occurred! I was so relieved, I can't even begin to tell you how much...' Having found her inspiration in the Harajuku girls, she clung to it like a life raft.

All of this begs the question of what Gwen was hoping to achieve in her solo career. What had she lacked in No Doubt that she hoped to change now? Or was it simply that she felt that she could go higher on her own than No Doubt could together? 'I never for one minute thought that I'd go solo,' she claims.

'It never crossed my mind, except when people would ask me. The real difference is that with No Doubt everything is a full collaboration, everybody has their vote and their energy: we're a real band. Nothing would be without all of us. Working with new collaborators and letting people in to try new melodies and new lyrical ideas was very hard. The idea was to be open and let my ego shut up and sit over in the corner and make something great based on a concept. That's why I don't really see this as a "solo" record in the typical sense. It's an art project; it's me collaborating with some different people to create something magical.' It is quite clear that this was not about Gwen's music: others provided that.

This was about manufacturing a stratospherically winning package: success, for success' sake might as well have been Iovine's stated aim. Even Gwen was quite aware that this album, in many ways, wasn't about her at all. 'Everyone keeps calling it a solo record and I keep calling it a dance record,' she told Blender. 'Cause if I was doing a solo record, that would be like, finally, me…finally this is the real Gwen Stefani. It's not that. This album is actually less of me than I've ever been before.'

The Cult of Gwen

The result was a dramatic departure from Gwen's previous musical fare as part of No Doubt. Gone was the ska that her earliest fans had hoped for (although No Doubt had also increasingly dropped this along the course of their musical evolution since 1987). Instead, she delivered a brand of 80s pop emulation quite different to any of her previous material. In addition, the introspective lyrics made famous by songs such as 'Don't Speak' had also largely been left by the wayside; there were few of the previous angst-ridden verses about the tortures that the likes of Tony and Gavin had inflicted on her. The quintessential Gwen was missing; instead, the lyrics were lighter, frothier and quite often entirely devoid of real meaning. There was certainly less substance, and the appeal was to a totally different fan base.

A huge amount of money was thrown at the project. What had started as a side-interest, while No Doubt were taking a hard-earned break, had turned into something else. Gwen was already famous, but *Love, Angel, Music, Baby* went global in 2005, pushing her right to the top. Her songs were rarely out of the Top 10 in the UK charts, and the album sold over 5 million copies.

images (c) Hewlett packard

There were other accolades which demonstrated just how popular L.A.M.B. was. 'Hollaback Girl' earned a world first. Despite the fact that few people had much of a clue what the title – let alone lyrics – referred to (and Gwen conceivably might be numbered amongst them), it was the most downloaded song in 2005, and first song in history to earn more than a million digital downloads.

L.A.M.B. was a sell-out, in both senses of the term. Gwen's solo career was a massive success, even compared to her earlier achievements with No Doubt. At the same time, though, that triumph came at some expense to her personal integrity. L.A.M.B. wasn't just about music – particularly Gwen's music. What she actually sang was the culmination of months of grinding, arduous partnership with some of the music industry's top names, not really her own material (although that did feature to some extent). But this wasn't just about music. This was about image. The result of Iovine's collaboration was to do nothing less than launch the personality cult of Gwen Stefani.

Convergence is a buzz-word in modern-day technology companies. Why have a separate mobile phone, camera, personal organiser and MP3 player, when you can combine them all into the same unit? The same is becoming true of other business interests. Iovine knew that Gwen was more than just a musical talent. Her image was worth a fortune. Anyone could see that from her previous music videos and public performances, although the full potential of that image had yet to be tapped. Then there was her clothing line, also titled L.A.M.B., which was attracting big interest in its own right. Doug Cole, director of Alliance Marketing and Entertainment for Hewlett Packard, summed it up (to drive home the point about convergence, he was talking about a 'Harajuku Lovers' digital camera that Gwen was involved in designing): 'Gwen epitomises the seamless blending of fashion, film, music and creativity, so it made perfect sense to partner with her to launch this limited edition personalised camera for customers.'

Her solo album was the convergence of all the things Cole mentioned. It was a re-invention of Gwen Stefani, a combination of music, fashion and personality, launched in an attractive package. Sceptics said that this wasn't really about Gwen at all: it was a slick production in which Gwen was just the vehicle for Iovine and co.'s tailored product. This was a radical departure from anything she'd previously been involved with but was all very neat, very well thought-through and, naturally, very, very lucrative.

Gwen has always maintained that she was a very passive person, who only got into singing because her brother pushed her into No Doubt. For several years, she went with the flow, until she discovered she could write for herself. That transformed her, and opened the door to a new phase in her life. One of the hardest things about working on *L.A.M.B.* was the level of co-operation with other artists, and particularly the problems she was having coming up with new material. This new move has often been dubbed a solo career, but in fact, it is anything but. Like an iceberg, with its outward glacial beauty, there was also an awful lot going on under the surface.

It is clear that Gwen found the whole process very tough. In some respects, her small idea of a solo sideline while No Doubt were taking a rest seems to have been hijacked and turned into something completely different. If she originally hoped to sing a few simple cover versions with Tony, Lovine had other ideas. She gave her project over to his crew, and between them they launched a product that was poles apart from the one she had envisaged when she first spoke to him about it, shortly after her wedding.

Whatever the process and sacrifices that led up to its release, *L.A.M.B.* was a phenomenal success. A catchy, if frequently vacuous strain of synth-pop, it had massive appeal – particularly to her teenage girl fan base. In 2005, everything came together at once for her, a backlog of projects seeing daylight and paying off: music, film, and fashion. Where did that leave No Doubt – unarguably Gwen's more serious incarnation? She was always careful to maintain that the band was only taking a break, not over for good. No Doubt is definitely not broken up,' she claimed. 'I don't even have plans to tour at this point; I don't see myself putting out a bunch of Gwen Stefani records. Who knows? I might have a baby and just want to stare at it all day and quit everything.' Every interview, that body clock seemed to tick louder…

Who knows? I might have a baby and just want to stare at it all day and quit everything.

Incident and Occident

One of the more perplexing aspects of Gwen's personality is her eclecticism. Like an overly-enthusiastic magpie, she will see something she likes and impulsively incorporate it into her style. In the past, this has led to some

stunning triumphs in the fashion arena as she creates wildly successful costumes from sometimes bizarrely disparate elements. On other occasions, it has bewildered and even upset the sensibilities of her fans and other onlookers. Gwen has rarely been overly concerned with making sense to her fans, as is clear from some of her song lyrics. (Her fans, for their part, don't seem too put off by this, 'Hollaback Girl' being a good case in point; few people seem to know or care exactly what a 'Hollaback Gir' is but it made music online history with its million digital-downloads.)

The latest whim to cause a series of double-takes wherever she goes are her idiosyncratic groupies, the Harajuku girls. They turn up alongside her in live appearances, music videos and promotional photos. Album *Love. Angel. Music. Baby.* – released in November 2004 – introduced this posse to an unsuspecting public. Gwen and her four Harajuku girls feature on the cover of this latest platinum-selling oeuvre in surreal, Dali-esque style, and so enamoured is she of these pint-sized Japanese fashionistas that they occur in the lyrics and videos of more than one of her songs. 'Harajuku Girls' is of course named after them.

'Rich Girl' is a dance remix of the *Fiddler on the Roof* classic, 'If I Was A Rich Man'. In the song's video – which takes place on a pirate ship, amid scenes of acrobatics and choreographed fighting – the alternately giggling and stern-faced Harajuku girls often take centre stage. This unashamed homage to all things materialistic includes the lines:

I'd get me four Harajuku girls to (uh huh)/ Inspire me and they'd come to my rescue/ I'd dress them wicked, I'd give them names (yeah)/ Love, Angel, Music, Baby/ Hurry up and come and save me.

And that, essentially, is what she has done.

So what, exactly, is a Harajuku girl, and why the intense fascination? These too-cool-for-school girls first came to Gwen's attention for their fashion sense. Harajuku is an area in Tokyo that became famous in the 1990s for its street performers and as a congregating area for wildly dressed teenagers. Now, it is known for its fashion boutiques, generally also aimed at young teenagers, and there is also a culture of individual fashion – crowds of school kids still gather there at weekends to shop, socialise and showcase their personal fashion styles.

Gwen learned of these hip young girls, expressing themselves in colourful and sometimes outrageous style, and was instantly impressed. Something about their playful experimentation, willingness to push the boundaries of fashion and sense of fun appealed to the same qualities in her; they became a powerful icon, an ideal of something she admired. Perhaps a sort of muse, as she has suggested a number of times. 'They really were just a fantasy,' she has maintained to bemused interviewers.

Fantasy, for most people, would be enough. But such was Gwen's faith in these girls that she decided to make them reality. World famous pop-stars can get away with such flights of fancy and, accordingly, auditions were held. Four Japanese girls – dancers by trade – were hired and transformed into the Harajuku posse that all her fans now associate with her.

Gwen insists that they began as figments of her imagination, which magically became reality as time passed. 'What people didn't seem to understand was that they really were just a fantasy,' she insisted in an interview with *The Independent*. 'Why didn't they realise that? Oh, sure, they're real now, but that's because they've become real, over time. But they weren't at first. Really, they weren't.'

The Independent's interviewer wasn't the only one to be nonplussed by Gwen's fantasy entourage. When she appeared as a guest on Jonathan Ross's BBC1 talk show, in November 2004, to promote her new album, her Harajuku troupe turned up with her too. Curious about her acolytes, Ross asked her why her entourage apparently consisted of unsmiling Asian women, dressed like Scottish schoolgirls. 'They're just imaginary. I just imagined them one day, and they were there,' she replied. How serious was she being? Ross didn't know, and reverted to type as a means of self-defence. With one of his trademark raised eyebrows, he suggested that one of the imaginary girls might like to give him a hand-job; after all, his wife could hardly complain if they didn't exist… Touché, Ms. Stefani.

Whilst some people found these whimsical extensions of Gwen's imagination fun, annoying or perplexing, others just thought they were downright offensive. It is one of the very rare occasions when Gwen has actively courted controversy. Members of the Asian community, in particular, were quick to criticise the whim/publicity stunt/eccentricity. (Which? No one seems to know for sure.) They were particularly angry about a rumour that the four had signed a contract never to speak English in public, even though they were perfectly capable of doing so. Instead, they had to maintain this image of unsmiling, uninterested schoolgirls. It also annoyed them that the quartet actually looked nothing like the kind of girls who really hung out in Harajuku: it was just a form of exploitation, of women and of a culture.

Shirley Tang, professor of Asian-American studies at UMass-Boston, was outspoken about what she saw as the perpetuation of an incorrect and damaging stereotype. 'It reminded me of that scene in Austin Powers with the Japanese women in the roles of sex symbols…men-pleasing roles,' she told the *Boston Herald*. She went on to say that western media generally puts Asian women into one of three categories: 'the super-sexy, exotic, diva slut; the submissive woman who will do anything to please a man; and the innocent little girl.' She forgot about the kung-fu goddess, but the point still stands that Gwen's use of the girls is hardly breaking any stereotypes. Anti-racism and sexism campaigner Sophia Kim maintained that this image was damaging. 'It's imposed this box on Asian women, on who we can be and can't be. And with non-Asian women and men, it shapes what they think about Asian women.' Mihi Ahn, of Salon.com, criticises, 'Stefani has taken the idea of Japanese street fashion and turned these women into modern-day geisha, contractually obligated to speak only Japanese in public, even though

it's rumoured they're just plain old Americans and their English is just fine... she's swallowed a subversive youth culture in Japan and barfed up another image of submissive giggling Asian women.'

So what exactly does Gwen (or her publicist) think she's doing? Ok, so the Harajuku girls have been a great inspiration to her, and have provided the impetus behind the whole L.A.M.B range of clothing as well as her music and videos. A tribute to that is only fair. **But actually hiring a bunch of Japanese dancers to follow her round like groupies? That's something, frankly, that we would expect from the likes of Michael Jackson** – showy, eccentric, impulsive and bound to get the PC brigade on the warpath.

But it's not as simple as that, as the myriad different responses to the quirky entourage prove. In fact, the whole thing really doesn't add up at all. Harajuku style is about expressing individuality; taking four Japanese women, putting them in school uniforms and having them fawn over her like lesbian concubines draws attention only to Gwen as the Queen bee. The Harajuku set – if, indeed, they can even be said to be a realistic reflection of their culture – are relegated to the status of human accessory, sacrificing their own attraction to promote that of the westerner. Gwen, in addition, is female herself (albeit a woman who at times presents herself as a bit tomboyish), so the argument that she is promoting the stereotype of Asian women as subservient men-pleasers doesn't really stand up. Plus, she's no doubt paying these girls a fortune to act as they do and given her track record on collaboration likely to be consulting them on the choreography of the act. Then, if you throw into the mix, the fact that she clearly isn't interested in racial stereotyping – the last song on the album, 'Long Way To Go', is actually about overcoming racism – it all starts to look a no-brainer. While Gwen herself may no be able to make the knock-down argument, the odds are she is just having fun dressing up the Barbie dolls in her new wardrobe.

Is it just possible that a part of the Harajuku girls' appeal for her is that they are so ridiculously over the top? Could there be just a little bit of satire here? Rappers, of course, use women as human accessories all the time (of course, in their case, although we tend to excuse it, some of them do mean it). And the likes of Madonna and J-Lo have huge entourages of personal attendants, dancers and musicians as well as technicians. Gwen could be sending them up by working the same entourage ticket?

Yet, the sad and cynical truth is that the whole thing is most likely a stunt, engineered by Interscope's publicity machine. *L.A.M.B.*, fashion and music, has been presented as an extension of Gwen's personality. That is what the solo album was all about: Gwen's fun-loving, musical, colourful, energetic character. When fans buy into that, they are signing up for a little bit of the Gwen Image, which has all the predictable commercial spin-offs. Art no longer has to be separate from the rest of life. It does not imitate life: it is life, or can be as long as the merch sales make the bottom line.

All this is painfully obvious from the trends in reporting and TV programmes. Audiences do not simply want to know about what celebrities are doing in their professional lives, but who they really are – what they do in their spare time, their families, friends, and relationships, where they go, what they wear. This has, in turn, given rise to celebrities who trade on that, peddling every detail of their lives to the media for the right price (the model Jordan being one extreme example – she even considered giving birth live on the internet on a pay-per-view basis. Nonetheless, Jordan remains devoted to her handicapped child...is there a heart of gold underneath the silicone?)

Gwen has never been mercenary, and there are details of her life that she prefers to keep out of the papers. Her marriage to Gavin is one such subject, and she is positively Trappist about her sex-life – and it is a refreshing change that a rock-star has a lifestyle that makes such an aspiration realistic. Still, her posse of Harajuku-girl followers is one part of her 'personality' – real or manufactured – that is fair game for the press. And they have done their job admirably. Without speaking so much as a word of English, without a single interview of their own, they have prompted a storm of publicity. Controversy or appreciation, it all amounts to more exposure, and record sales have certainly not suffered for it.

Love. Angel. Music... Baby?

Despite such bizarre choices of retinue, Gwen has resolutely managed to avoid the kind of mud that gets thrown around superstars like herself. In fact, as far as rock chicks go, she has got to be one of the cleanest around. There are no bar-hopping, bed-hopping, coke-snorting or paparazzi-beating incidents for the hacks to get their noses into – all the more surprising, given her in-your-face sexuality oozes from every performance.

Gwen has only ever had two 'real' relationships, as she puts it (presumably here a euphemism for sexual partners): the first with No Doubt's bassist and her co-songwriter, Tony Kanal, and the second with her husband, Bushman Gavin Rossdale. She has hinted at her dissatisfaction with the situation, which partly comes down to the expectations of women. 'In my next life I am going to be a guy and I'm going to be a complete slut,' she once said. In addition, she admits to just one above-the waist petting incident, with the keyboard player of 80s ska/funk/reggae/rock band, Fishbone. She told *Bliss* magazine: 'I once made out with the keyboard player from Fishbone and he tried to take advantage of the situation, and I was not about to let him.'

> In my next life I am going to be a guy and I'm going to be a complete slut.

Fishbone were one of Gwen's childhood idols, so presumably she felt obliged to let him inside her bra but certainly not her knickers. The band has had more than one keyboardist, but Gwen does not elaborate on which one was so honoured. Such a chaste encounter, though, is hardly the stuff of celebrity kiss 'n' tell and, as this looks to be the sum total of her skeletons in the closet, there will never be any salacious revelations to come. At school, she claims she never dated. 'I was too shy to go on dates,' she told *Female First* magazine. Instead, she would invent fictitious partners to deter would-be admirers.

If she were any more squeaky-clean, only dogs would be able to hear her. Gwen has therefore managed to avoid many of the rumour-mill's damaging attacks that her peers take as a hazard of the job. Unfortunately, her husband had not been so self-controlled, and she was painfully introduced to the sharp end of celebrity scandal in 2004 when Gavin hit the tabloids amid news of a newly-discovered love-child.

This oversight goes back 17 years to a time when he was a carefree young member of the infamous Primrose Hill Set, rubbing shoulders and exchanging bodily fluids with the likes of Sadie Frost, Jude Law, Pearl Lowe, Kate Moss... At the time, the teenage Pearl was pursuing a career in modelling after a heady period of self-discovery. 'I went off at 14 and had lots of tattoos and body piercings and dyed my hair black. My parents thought I was a freak. I got expelled from school then was spotted by a model agent and was signed up,' she once told the *Mail on Sunday*. She didn't mention her fling with Gavin.

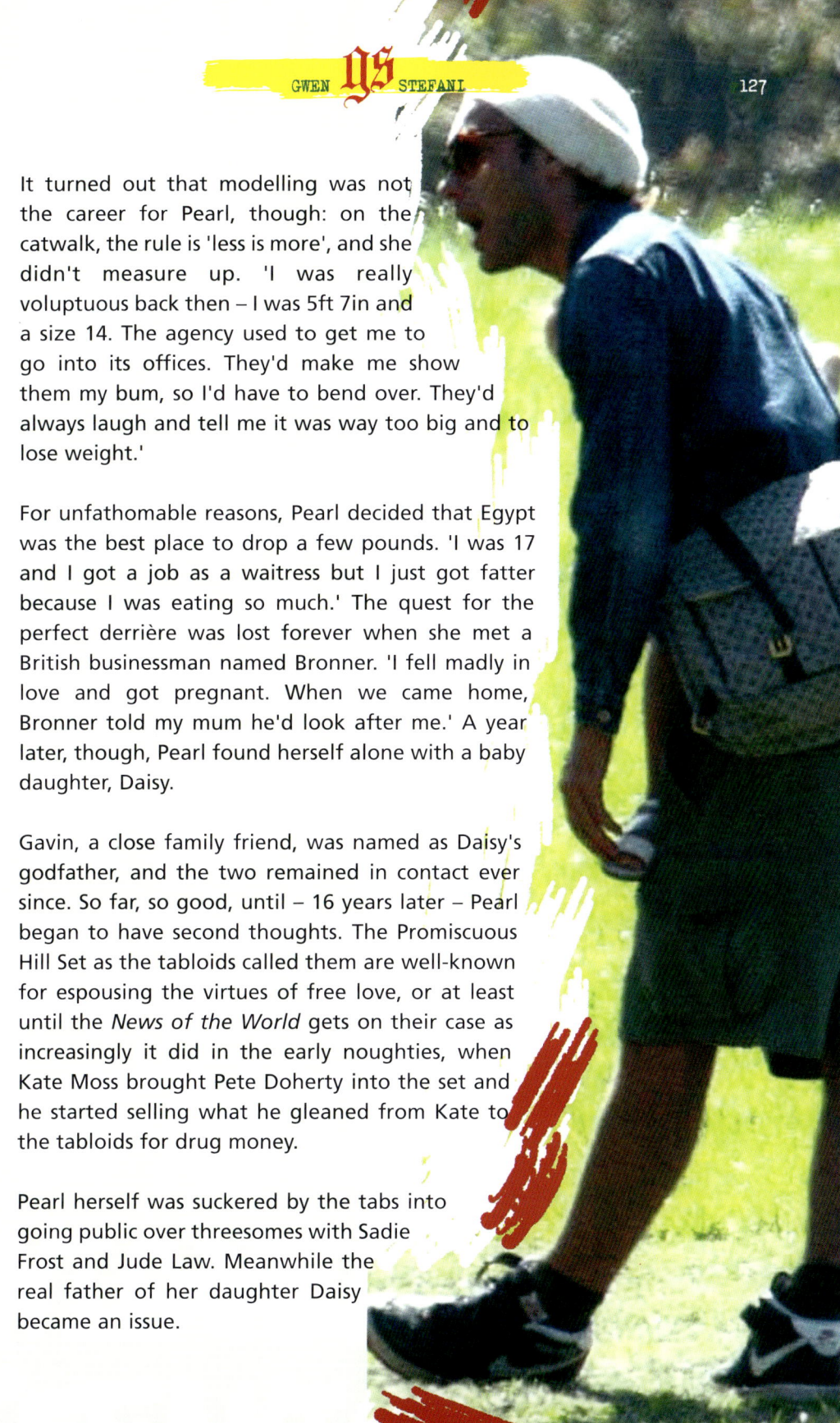

It turned out that modelling was not the career for Pearl, though: on the catwalk, the rule is 'less is more', and she didn't measure up. 'I was really voluptuous back then – I was 5ft 7in and a size 14. The agency used to get me to go into its offices. They'd make me show them my bum, so I'd have to bend over. They'd always laugh and tell me it was way too big and to lose weight.'

For unfathomable reasons, Pearl decided that Egypt was the best place to drop a few pounds. 'I was 17 and I got a job as a waitress but I just got fatter because I was eating so much.' The quest for the perfect derrière was lost forever when she met a British businessman named Bronner. 'I fell madly in love and got pregnant. When we came home, Bronner told my mum he'd look after me.' A year later, though, Pearl found herself alone with a baby daughter, Daisy.

Gavin, a close family friend, was named as Daisy's godfather, and the two remained in contact ever since. So far, so good, until – 16 years later – Pearl began to have second thoughts. The Promiscuous Hill Set as the tabloids called them are well-known for espousing the virtues of free love, or at least until the *News of the World* gets on their case as increasingly it did in the early noughties, when Kate Moss brought Pete Doherty into the set and he started selling what he gleaned from Kate to the tabloids for drug money.

Pearl herself was suckered by the tabs into going public over threesomes with Sadie Frost and Jude Law. Meanwhile the real father of her daughter Daisy became an issue.

According to *Star* magazine, which published the lurid details of what inexorably followed, Gwen had always been uneasy about Gavin's friendship with Pearl, and had even asked him to stay away from her. Then, shortly after the couple had married, she started asking awkward questions. Several people had taken to remarking on the uncanny likenesses between Daisy and Gavin. Gwen decided that the direct approach was the best, and asked him outright if he was the father. *Star*'s source claimed that Gavin 'swore blind that he had never had sex with Pearl'.

Pearl, under pressure from the tabs, decided some damage limitation was the order of the day and she asked Gavin to take a DNA test, a request that apparently developed into an exchange of legal letters. In the end according to the *Mail on Sunday*, it was Pearl's current partner, Supergrass drummer Danny Goffey, who convinced Gavin to take the test 'out of curiosity'. When the results landed on Pearl's doormat in October 2004, there it was in black and white: godfather Gavin was actually Daisy's dad.

Gwen was devastated to find out that she was unwittingly a stepmother, and incandescent about Gavin lying to her. Her husband's past had always been an exposed nerve in their relationship: before that Gavin had been linked to various other singers, including former All Saint Natalie Appleton – 'an absolute circumcised dog' was one description – and Andrea Corr, lead singer of the Celtic-pop band The Corrs. Gwen was plagued with suspicions that Gavin's taste for groupies had never really gone away. 'I'm in a band and I know exactly what goes on backstage,' she said. 'I wish I had a little leash to walk him around.'

As with many aspects of Gwen's life, her misgivings about Gavin had previously found a voice in her music. In an interview with *AOL* in 2000, she spoke briefly about the meaning of the song 'Bathwater'. 'It kind of has to do with the idea that somebody ever had any kind of lovers before you, and the idea that they have any kind of past or history…but you still, even though you hate the idea or loathe the idea that they ever were with anybody else, you still find yourself – I don't know – indulging in their love…"Bathwater" is maybe like somebody's dirty water, their dirty old baggage, something like that.' It wasn't particularly eloquent, and it wasn't too flattering either.

Whilst Gavin's Lothario lifestyle remains in the past, the knowledge of his secret fling and subsequent child with Pearl Lowe was understandably a bone

of contention in their marriage. Recriminations inevitably followed his breach of trust and they split more than once with only Gwen leaving the door open for Gavin to slink back in. At least he did but the distress got to her: she cut short an interview with Radio 1 when talking about the incident. What hurt her most was they had no children of their own: Gwen had been outspoken in the past about the realities of her age, her ticking biological clock and hopes for a family. What rubbed salt in the wound was Pearl took legal action against Gavin for child support.

A Pregnant Pause

Family had been on Gwen's mind for a while now. When her wedding effectively sealed the deal with Gavin and left her devoid of relationship issues to write lyrics about, one of the things that came to the fore was her desire for a baby. After all, she had put it on hold for a long time – a child was hardly compatible with the world-touring rock-goddess status she had been enjoying since 1995 – and something she couldn't afford to delay for much longer. It is something she has never made a great secret of; at the age of 17 when she started out with Tony, it was all she hoped for out of life. 'I've always wanted to be a mother,' she told *Marie Claire* in 2005. 'I was hanging with my nephew the other day, and he's like a frickin' Twinkie he's so delicious.' Great though motherhood would be, there was more to it than her own hopes. Gavin and her own body clock were factored in there too. 'But it's kind of not up to me. I've been on this journey, and I don't want to be too greedy about what's going to come next. I'll be really happy when it happens.' She was 35, and becoming more and more acutely aware that, if it didn't happen soon, it might never.

As early as 2000, she had been singing of her uncertain relationship with Rossdale, 'I always thought I'd be a mom/ Sometimes I wish for a mistake/ The longer that I wait the more selfish that I get/ You seem like you'd be a good dad' ('Simple Kind of Life'). As time went on, that feeling only got more intense. 'What You Waiting For?' – the first song on *L.A.M.B.* – expressed her growing concerns in typical blunt style: '…How did the years go by? Now it's only me. (Tick, tock, tick, tock.) Like a cat in heat stuck in a moving car… Your moment will run out cause of your sex chromosome.' The fact that Gavin had already managed to have a child, and with so little effort (or planning) on his part, only made it worse.

Conceiving wasn't as easy as she'd been led to believe. 'It hasn't happened, and that's something that isn't in my control,' she said in 2005. 'I'd like it to happen, of course I would, but I have an amazing husband and the most fulfilling, creative career I ever dreamed of, so I'm not complaining.' Complaining or not, it was clear that she was getting desperate.

Late in 2005, she finally got her life-long wish. At a concert in Florida in December, at the end of her US tour, she announced her pregnancy to the crowds. As the audience sang along to 'Crash' (a heavily R&B influenced number that pushed the boundaries of even her mix-and-match attitude to music), she called out, 'I want you to say it loud enough so the baby hears it.' It was a mistake: she and Gavin had agreed to keep it quiet for as long as possible to avoid the inevitable media circus that would result. 'I'm really horrible with secrets,' she told the *Los Angeles Times* afterwards. 'It's amazing we kept it quiet as long as we did, I suppose. There are so many things that are going to change, you know?'

She was right. Her pregnancy had come at the absolute peak of her career. There was no way she could maintain the pace and schedule she had grown used to. She would also be waving farewell to her athletic figure, shortly to go beyond the reach of any exercise regime. 'It's the best gift, but I do look at my stage clothes and wonder if I will ever get into them again,' she commented. Determined to look stylish whatever her shape, she spent a fortune on maternity wear and baby clothes. On one shopping spree, she blew £13,000 in Elias & Grace, a classy London boutique. According to a shop assistant: 'It was an incredible haul of gear. Gwen loved the Petit Bateau kids' clothes. She was holding them up to Gavin and saying, "Aww, so cute. I want this in my size." She was also holding up scratch mittens and saying, "Look – so tiny!" She took pretty much the whole range in various ages.'

Gwen had hoped that pregnancy wouldn't interfere too much with her schedule. After all, with her solo career heading skywards, there was a lot at stake. 'I thought I was going to be one of those Mother Nature girls. I figured, I'll just squeeze it out, 'cause I'm really strong and I work out and stuff,' she told *Elle*. But continuing with the tour wasn't as easy as she'd hoped. 'I would be seriously crying before I went onstage. I didn't know how I was going to get through the tour, putting on nine costume changes on a stage in front of 12,000 people every night. And I didn't want people to know...I didn't want it to become the Gwen Circus Freak Show: Watch It Grow Onstage.'

Kingston James McGregor Rossdale was born by caesarean section on May 26 at the Cedars-Sinai Medical Center, Los Angeles. He weighed seven pounds and five ounces. Gwen took to motherhood instantly, helped by a big group of friends. 'There's this huge team of us always hanging out together, so he gets to see the same people every day,' she told *USA Today*. 'And he's this very cool, chilled-out little guy. He's just like another person, except that he's super-cute and super-entertaining.'

Gavin thought fatherhood was fantastic, too. 'It's great! I love it!' he enthused. It wasn't long before the family was spotted with another celebrity family, as Kingston enjoyed a play date with Angelina Jolie and Brad Pitt's new baby, Shiloh. Quick to immerse himself in the celebrity lifestyle, Kingston has also been spotted kitted out in designer baby wear and L.A.M.B. clothes.

Sickly Sweet

Not long after Kingston was born, Gwen announced her intention to have another child – the biological clock still being the motivating factor. 'I pray that I can have another baby,' she said to *Elle*. 'I mean, it's such a miracle to have one. And there's so much I still want to do, because who knows? Things could be a lot harder a few years from now. I mean, I'm not at the beginning of my career. I'm on a ticking clock. And I don't want to miss anything.' Baby or not, her career was showing little sign of slowing down. Starting a family had barely been a hiccup in her schedule. Touring for *L.A.M.B.* in December 2005, it would be less than a year before her second solo album came out – only six months after Kingston's birth.

Initially, Gwen had not expected to do this. As it turned out, there had been unused material from *L.A.M.B.*, and she couldn't bear to see it go to waste. 'I never intended to do another solo record,' she told Adelaide Now. 'It's, like, kind of embarrassing talking about it. I had a couple of amazing leftover tracks from the last one...but I wanted to have a baby. Now I have both. I'm just going with the flow.'

The impression given is that it all just happened around her, but that wasn't the case. Apart from actually putting the material together, performing on-stage again required that she regain her old figure – against the clock. 'That was one of the hardest things for me – the pressure of, "OK, I need to get into

shape so that I can put this record out,"' she told *USA Today*. 'If I didn't have that pressure, I don't think I would have gotten the baby weight off so quickly.' In the madness of getting everything ready in time, as well as looking after a baby, Kingston was actually a source of sanity. 'He's pretty rad. Kingston is so chill. He goes with me everywhere, 'cause I'm still nursing,' she said at the beginning of 2007. 'He's been to every studio in L.A., New York, London. He lives up to his name – total Rasta boy. He gives me real balance. You can go 100 miles an hour, but you have to stop to hang out with him.'

Most of the work for *The Sweet Escape* was carried out in the months immediately after Kingston's birth. Gwen was working with the same crew who had helped make *L.A.M.B.* such a success. There was also some new talent, including rapper Akon, who appears in one of the tracks. The style of this second album was very different again. 'The last one was a total dance record,' she said. 'Not serious, very light. This one is way different. The inspiration for this one is "it doesn't have a direction" which makes it very modern.' Gwen also started working back round to her roots, the confessional style that made No Doubt so famous. 'On the last record I was trying to be a bit more balanced, trying to play more character roles and be light-hearted. I fell back into my normal patterns on this one. I don't edit myself. I'm not scared to share myself with people.'

As far as material went, finding Mr Right and having a child had robbed her of valuable song lyrics. In *Sweet Escape*, she has to fall back on marital discontent and other minor irritations for inspiration. 'It's your fault you didn't shut the refrigerator/ Maybe that's the reason I've been acting so cold?' Other songs displayed a bizarrely eclectic mix of influences – even more so than usual. The four Harajuku girls naturally featured again, this time with Gwennabe-blond hair. When the album was released on Dec 4, 2006, it was to very mixed reviews. Sceptics were found even amongst those who had loved her solo debut.

One song that polarised the fans and critics was 'Wind It Up', which drew heavily on *The Sound of Music*'s 'Lonely Goatherd' and incorporated repeated yodelling. 'Beyond flawed...irritatingly bad,' wrote music critic Jim deRogatis of the *Chicago Sun-Time*s, 'an even more horrible, fingernails-on-a-chalkboard ditty.' This was representative of reviewers, who particularly despised *The Sound of Music* sample – though the public vindicated Gwen's judgement in the charts.

Rolling Stone had the best word on the album: 'The sorriest thing to happen to the goatherd community since the Swiss cops cracked down on livestock-fondling. Unfortunately, it sets the tone for the whole album – she's doing the same thing she did last time, except it's not as much fun.'

Others were less unforgiving, citing the album's catchy tunes and signature heart-on-sleeve lyrics as proof of success, albeit not to the standard of *L.A.M.B.* The sheer diversity of style that alienated some critics was also a draw to others. *The Guardian* wrote, 'Pharrell Williams' production and Stefani's fizzy personality make for an unexpected Christmas treat.' However, outright praise generally centred on specific songs, whilst admitting that the rest of the album contained more than its fair share of lemons. One way or another, *The Sweet Escape* shifted 243,000 copies in the first week of sales in the US alone. Gwen's new World Tour was scheduled for April 2007, starting in North America.

After that? Her options are open, though now she has got her solo career out of her system, she is keen finally to return to her band mates in No Doubt. 'I guess we'll have to wait and see,' she says.

ROCK STEADY

Looking back at her life from the beginning of this new chapter, Gwen can afford some satisfaction. She has been performing now for almost 20 years, and has come a very long way – even by the standards of a highly demanding industry. Considering that she didn't know what she wanted to do with her life, she has had an amazing career. It still doesn't add up to her that a fat, dorky kid who didn't have many friends at school and whose brother was her main source of motivation could have made it as a star in so many areas. As she once put it herself, way back in 1996 when she was just hitting the headlines, 'I never thought that me, this loser from Anaheim, could have any effect on anyone. I never had any creativity or anything. Then, suddenly, I'm what everyone is looking at. It's such a strange thing, but it's so exciting… Like I would talk about Madness, they're going to talk about No Doubt? How cool is that!?'

Now, of course, with a solo career, a fashion line and a film, the modest level of success she had then has paled in comparison. For a kid who always thought she was lazy, her life has been second to none.

Gwen – in all her facets – is a fusion of many different influences. Her music, her fashion, and her personality are all tributes to diversity and eclecticism. Part of her is 40s movie icon; part of her is tomboy cool. Part of her is a wife and mother; part of her is a sex-symbol who is unafraid to exploit a fantastic figure. Part of her is little-girl-lost; part of her can sing about moving on and refusing to conform to sexist stereotypes.

But who is Gwen Stefani, underneath all of this apparent conflict? For all her rock-chick image, it is clear where her heart is. Some things haven't changed in the two decades she's been in the business. She is still a clean-living girl with basically simple concerns: her husband and now family mean the world to her. Whatever expression her personality finds through fashion, music and other outlets, that is unlikely to change. As *The Independent* put it, Gwen 'knows how to act the good girl while dressing the rebel.' She enjoys the energy of her performances, and they provide a powerful outlet for her angst, joys and grievances, but that is not who she is. Put simply, she is a sheep in wolf's

clothing. Garage singer Shirley Manson, who epitomises the 'skank appeal' of which Gwen has been accused, has known her for ten years. 'Very benign and wholesome,' is her assessment. But just because Gwen hasn't let go of her morals and strict upbringing doesn't make her weak; 'underneath lurks an incredible toughness and powerful directness.' Getting to where she is now hasn't been an easy ride and that aspect of her character is a result of the tough times she endured. She has had to deal with the suicide of a close friend, the loss of her brother and mentor from the band, and the break-up of a long-term relationship.

Those early days in No Doubt had a huge impact on her. In the beginning, she was uncertain and timid about singing at all; now, she appears to be a different person entirely. But her outward, brash confidence still masks the insecurities she has always felt. Gwen takes criticism very much to heart, and one of the difficult things about being so famous is the level of sniping she has to endure. 'I have a hard time reading stuff on my Web site,' she said by way of example to *Cosmopolitan*. 'I've actually been considering shutting it down because it's such a great opportunity for people to bag on you. It feels like the more I'm out there in the public eye, the more criticism I get. You need to have confidence – that's what it takes to walk out there and sing a song in front of a huge group of people. But the criticism hurts, and it fucks with you.'

In many fans' opinions, one of the greatest criticisms is that Gwen has sold out. Having made it big with No Doubt, she traded on this fame and used it to launch a solo career. Whereas many artists go solo to showcase their unique talents and individual style, the accusation is that Gwen did so simply to make money, and that the result is less about her and more about using her to promote a different product. She allowed Interscope the freedom to take her project away from her, replacing it with a popular but misleading substitute.

One reviewer, unimpressed at the concoction of influences on *L.A.M.B.*, reduced its sound to 'Top 40 in a blender,' and the constitution of Gwen's character to '45% fashion sense, 30% acquisition of wealth, 12% posturing, 10% getting off, 2% conscience, 1% memory of selling out.' *Sweet Escape* attracted worse criticism, and if she continues down the same route, she can expect more of that in the future. Fortunately, that doesn't seem to be her intention.

This is a natural time in Gwen's life to take a step back and decide what is going to happen next. In one sense, she has gone an extremely long way. In another, she has come full circle and is back where she started 20 years ago: a girl looking forward to a life with kids and the man she loves. And, as in those early days, No Doubt seems to loom large in her future. She claims not to be planning a third album. 'I don't think there's going to be another solo one,' she told Adelaide Now. 'I feel pretty completed after this one. It's kind of, like, taken me on a road back to No Doubt.' When she finally reaches the end of the line with music, she has a backup plan. 'The idea is to do fashion for the rest of my life; I hate saying it because if it folds everyone will know how much it hurts.'

Gwen has always maintained, 'I'm just an Orange County girl from a loving family making music with my friends. It's not really that big of a deal.' Her most dedicated fans will hope that she holds true to this, and does indeed go back to her roots with the ska-fusion band, No Doubt. That seems to be the place that offered her the greatest opportunities of self-expression, and the arena in which she really thrived. It is also a great part of her history, and it will be difficult for her to let that go.

Gwen has many options open to her, including music, fashion and film. The future is bright for her, full of opportunities. For the moment, though, she can afford to relax. No doubt she will, in time, move on to other successes. For now, with a husband and a baby, and with an already incredible career behind her, she has everything she has ever wanted... Well except being a slut but that will have to wait until another life.

Sometimes you have to sacrifice your performance for high heels.
GWEN STEFANI